PRODUCTIVE, SUCCESSFUL YOU!

End Procrastination by Making Anxiety Work for You Rather Than Against You

Jenny C. Yip, Psy.D., ABPP

A Strategic Cognitive Behavioral Institute Book

This publication is intended to provide information on the subject matter covered. The purpose is not to render psychological or other professional services.

Cover design and illustrations by Marianne Epstein.
Edited by Patty Park.

ISBN: 0615952747
ISBN 13: 9780615952741
Library of Congress Control Number: 2014931186
Strategic Cognitive Behavioral Institute Book
Los Angeles, California

To my hardworking and devoted parents:

For your endless sacrifices to ensure my livelihood,
and for modeling the discipline of productivity and success.

This book reflects the skills I've learned through them.

ACKNOWLEDGMENTS

The inspiration behind this book belongs to those patients and students whom I have had the privilege to teach and work with over the years. They gave me the reason to put these tools to paper. Without understanding their struggles with anxiety, perfectionism, and procrastination, I would not have even realized the skills that I've become accustomed to and taken for granted because of my upbringing. I thank them for their patience as I learned through them, and hope I have provided them with useful tools for tackling their challenges.

I owe a debt of gratitude to Dr. Charles Mansueto for his guidance, kindness, and life lessons. He has been a constant mentor throughout my career, providing me with the foundation that has shaped my life's work. Thank you to Dr. Edith Packer and Dawn Michelle Wilson for the direction and recommendations that fortified the completion of this book. A special thanks to Marianne Epstein who brought the caveman to life, and for enduring this lengthy, tedious process despite my meticulous requests. A sincere appreciation to Dr. Sarah Haider and Kay Ramsey for stepping in and holding the fort to allow me the mental space to write. I am especially thankful to all the staff at the Renewed Freedom Center for their patience with my absence during my writing days.

A heartfelt gratitude to my better half, Marc, for his devotion, relentless encouragement, and constant reminders to balance work and play. Above all, I am appreciative of my family and friends for their kindness, understanding, and tolerance of my workaholic nature. It would not have been possible to write this book without their sentiments and endless support.

CONTENTS

INTRODUCTION

"Dare to live the life you have dreamed for yourself.
Go forward and make your dreams come true."
—Ralph Waldo Emerson

Welcome to Your New Productive Lifestyle

Do you procrastinate? Do you put off projects until the last minute, just to find yourself pulling all-nighters to meet morning deadlines? Does your work seem to overwhelm you? Do your goals often seem unattainable or beyond your grasp? Do you ever feel unmotivated, uninspired, or just plain lazy? In other words, do you … P-R-O-C-R-A-S-T-I-N-A-T-E? If you answered yes to any of these questions, then you've come to the right place.

You will learn how to turn your procrastination into productivity with these detailed step-by-step instructions. Be warned, though: If you are looking for some magical solution that can simply turn you into a productive person, this book is not for you. No such solution exists, and attempting to find one will be even less productive (and potentially more expensive) than procrastinating. You will have to be motivated enough to put these tools to action in order to reap the benefits. Of course, just by reading this, you've shown that you *are* motivated to become more productive!

Procrastination comes in all sorts of shapes and sizes. Some people are just underwhelmed and disinterested at the tedious task at hand, and would rather spend their limited time on earth on more rewarding activities. Other people become completely overwhelmed by the unrealistically high standards that they set for themselves, and prefer to avoid anything short of perfection. Still others are crippled simply by perceiving ordinary tasks as mountainous missions in which the path toward the end result becomes buried and lost. No matter the reason, there's one thing in common with all forms of procrastination: ANXIETY.

As a licensed psychologist and an anxiety expert, this is a frequent problem that I've seen all too often from my patients, young and old. Goals

that are impractical or that are only met with excessive effort, kill motivation. Unfortunately, an absence of drive will surely result in avoidance and procrastination. Consequently, the lack of productivity further leads to guilt, shame, anxiety, and low self-esteem. Why would anyone want to engage in a boring task that will require a great deal of time, you ask? Or who would want to tackle an endeavor that requires an insurmountable level of energy? The answer depends on how you're looking at the problem. And fortunately, there is a solution that has worked for many of my patients who have acquired and practiced the tools you're about to learn.

The first part of this book will teach you about the fight-or-flight response, which you will use as the motivation to enhance your productivity. Next, you will learn to identify and neutralize cognitive distortions – thinking traps that are the enemy of productivity and that prevent you from being productive. Once you better understand the enemy, you will learn a variety of tools to defeat procrastination and become a proactive, successful individual. I will start each section of the book by describing the purpose and function of the tool, and explain how to apply the tool to your daily life. Each section is followed by anecdotes that will detail how some of my patients have put these same tools to action in order to achieve their goals and overcome procrastination habits. It is my hope that these stories will help you relate to the experience of implementing these tools and tackling potential obstacles. Of course, all names and classifying information have been changed to protect these individuals' identities. Finally, worksheets in the appendix section will provide you with concrete examples, and guide you to apply each specific tool. These resources will help you stay on target to acquire the skills necessary for productive habits in the long run.

By understanding and practicing these tools, you too can learn to overcome procrastination. Whether you are trying to meet deadlines efficiently, balance work and play, maintain a new exercise program, get mundane household chores done, or even complete that manuscript that's been on the backburner for years, you will be on your way. With the right attitude, dedication, and the tools outlined in this book, you can reach your goals and become the success you've always known that you can be. This is your journey ... Make the most of it!

SECTION I

"Whether you think that you can,
or that you can't, you are usually right."
—Henry Ford

Understanding What Motivates You

Motivation is the key instrument to any productive effort. Motivation is also dependent on morale – your belief in yourself to achieve your established goals.

Certain factors contribute to morale and motivation that can lead to either procrastination or productivity. More specifically, the fight-or-flight response has an indirect effect while cognitive distortions have a direct effect. You will learn in the following chapters how both of these factors affect your drive and motivation. In turn, learning to make the most of what motivates you will increase your productivity. In this section, we'll look at reasons why we all procrastinate and how to avoid these barriers.

CHAPTER ONE

"It's not events, but our opinions about them,
which cause us suffering."
—Epictetus

Jenny C. Yip, Psy.D., ABPP

The Fight-or-Flight Response: Your Enemy or Secret Weapon?

You feel your heart palpitating. Your breathing intensifies. Your muscles begin to tremble and your chest tightens. We have all experienced it before, whether through the sudden rush of nearly avoiding a car accident or the much-sought-after thrills of extreme sports, such as skydiving. Fear, anxiety, stress, excitement – whatever you choose to label it – this is your fight-or-flight response in action. Though you may not realize it, this very same response propels you to finish that draft by six in the morning, rush to get to work on time each day, or even complete simple household tasks like washing your dishes or mowing your lawn. If you want to overcome procrastination, you first must understand how the fight-or-flight response motivates you to act. And you must see how it is always your choice whether this collection of sensations is your friend or foe.

When you talk about anxiety, fear, or stress, you are communicating your subjective experience of the objective biological fight-or-flight response. Depending on whom you ask, skydiving could be either a horribly terrifying or a wonderfully exciting experience. Everyone who skydives experiences a similar, objective fight-or-flight biological response, most noted for its sudden "adrenaline rush." However, your mind interprets these biological events subjectively; while I might find the experience enthralling, you might think quite differently.

From where did the biological fight-or-flight response come? As Charles Darwin's theory of natural selection states, organisms with more effective adaptations will be more capable of surviving and producing offspring. Having bodies that respond quickly and instinctually to threats increases your chances of adapting and surviving. A primitive human, for example, when faced with a sabertooth tiger, needs to either stand his ground and fight, or run for his life (hence the term "fight-or-flight"). What would happen to a caveman if he simply stood there when the sabertooth appeared? He would be lunch, because his body did not respond suitably to this threat. A caveman whose body did give him a near-instantaneous signal would have been more likely to survive such encounters and have descendants. The fight-or-flight response, developed over hundreds of thousands of years, is part of the evolved human body – a complex and powerful machine equipped for survival. Some variation of the fight-or-flight response is found in every single animal.

In humans, the response has a few common, objective biological sensations. These occur whenever your fight-or-flight response engages, which can happen in almost any type of situation – even if there is no immediate threat to your life. The anxiety you might feel when you procrastinate is simply your fight-or-flight alarm. This very response can be employed as a trigger to motivate you in accomplishing your goals. A powerful dose of this biological response is what can make cramming at the last minute somewhat possible. The next time you find yourself procrastinating, try to notice some of these physiological signs of your fight-or-flight trigger at work:

- Increased heart rate
- Headaches, muscle tension
- Lightheadedness, nausea
- Shaking or restlessness
- Tightness in the chest
- Shortness of breath
- Dry mouth or lump in the throat
- Tingling or numbness in parts of the body
- Sweaty or clammy skin
- Stomach problems or sudden diarrhea
- Flushes or chills

If the fight-or-flight response is pushing you to accomplish your goals, then why do you procrastinate? Procrastination occurs when you are either bored and underwhelmed from a lack of the fight-or-flight trigger, or completely overwhelmed with an extremely excessive fight-or-flight response that you've misinterpreted. To achieve productivity, you must learn how to make use of the most adequate level of the fight-or-flight energy that will motivate you to take action.

Fight-or-Flight Thermometer

10	Overextension, straining energy, breaking point, procrastination
9	Distraught, distressing energy, overwhelmed, procrastination
8	Threatening, excessive energy, maximum productivity, cramming
7	Alarm, superior energy, high productivity
6	Warning, intense energy, enhanced productivity
5	Alert, moderate energy, modest productivity
4	Caution, mild energy, minimal productivity
3	Aware, diminutive energy, negligible productivity
2	Relaxed, complacent, no productivity
1	Bored, underwhelmed, no productivity, procrastination
0	Dead, no reflex

In modern times, many perceived threats are not dire. When a saber-tooth tiger is moving toward you, you must act immediately; delaying even one second can mean the difference between life and death. However, if you have a week to finish a proposal for a client, the threat is less urgent. How many times have you said to yourself, "I can finish this tomorrow; there's plenty of time," only to find yourself stressing at the last minute to meet your deadline? Unlike primitive man facing the sabertooth tiger, you always have tomorrow to start your work. Well … maybe. At least you have the option of telling yourself that, without becoming lunch to a wild animal. However, as long as you use that excuse, you will always push off your deadlines until the last minute. And while you may not lose your life, when you procrastinate chronically, you will lose a degree of self-esteem and end up feeling negative about yourself and your life.

You may say to yourself, "I've always pushed off my deadlines until the last minute, and it's never been an issue. I still end up finishing my work on time. So why not just wait till tomorrow?" Certainly, you may have tomorrow to finish your work. However, are you truly fulfilled when doing the bare minimum, and always just getting by? If so, you would probably be sitting in front of the TV watching "Gilligan's Island" reruns instead of reading this book. Simply doing the minimum required, rather than motivating yourself to set and achieve goals, will lead to mediocrity and stagnation. You will not reach your optimal potential, and instead, will minimize the possibilities in your life. However, achieving goals by maximizing your effort without procrastination will lead to increased self-esteem and motivation for further productive efforts, because you show yourself what you're truly capable of.

If you want to thrive personally as well as professionally, then you need to learn the skill of establishing long-term, self-imposed goals. The tools that I will introduce in a few pages will help you understand how to accomplish this. You may also want to keep in mind that for every second you spend not working toward your goals, someone else out there is putting in that time. If you want to be a successful person, then you need to start competing at the level of other *successful* people. Though your deadline may not be as pressing as an encounter with a sabertooth, it could still be a key to your future as a successful and independent individual.

This raises an argument that has been presented to me many times: "I work better under pressure." The problem with this statement is that in one sense, it just might be true. Why? Because of your fight-or-flight response! When the deadline for a project looms closer, you feel a much more pressing need to complete the task. The danger is more imminent and your need to survive feels more acute. Because of this, you may finish in a matter of hours what you once thought could take a week or longer to accomplish. However, just because you are producing a product does not mean that product is as high in quality as it could be if you had used your adrenaline levels effectively.

In fact, when your biological fight-or-flight response is running strong, it decreases your ability for analytical thinking and focuses your body and mind toward simple, intuitive responses. While this may be fine for surviving an encounter with a sabertooth, it is not the best way to generate the intellectual products that have serious value in today's world. Could you write a quality proposal while running a marathon? This is essentially your predicament when you use last-minute pressure to generate work. You are not functioning at your highest intellectual capacity, and your work will reveal that fact and reflect poorly on you. Is a last-minute rush job what you want the world to see when judging you? Working in this manner also wreaks havoc on your body when pushing it up and down to extremes. This produces long-term stress with all of the associated mental and physical health effects that come with it. If you learn to use your fight-or-flight energy consistently as a trigger that motivates action, then you'll stop ending up in this last-minute predicament. Your body and mind will thank you for it!

PERSONAL ANECDOTES

Raquel – 12yo, Piano Prodigy

When Raquel first learned to play the piano, she was five years old. Despite having played the piano successfully at various recitals for seven consecutive years, she continued to experience intense anxiety during the week leading up to each recital. She described feeling such jitters when thinking about having to perform in front of an audience, that it was difficult to keep her fingers from shaking and sweating. She worried about missing a key during the recitals, losing her place while playing the notes, or blanking and forgetting the music altogether. Although she had been able to push herself through each recital, her parents noticed an increase in time spent procrastinating rather than actual practicing. According to Raquel, playing the piano had become increasingly unbearable as each piece of music became more difficult to play. She was no longer having fun, and spent more time worrying about giving a perfect performance than enjoying the activity.

Raquel interpreted her body's natural fight-or-flight trigger as negative anxiety. She perceived the possibility of performing poorly in front of an audience as the threatening sabertooth tiger. To help her understand the utility of this fight-or-flight adrenaline, I asked her to imagine having to play a new piece of music at her recital the next day without feeling any pressure at all. No one would care or judge, and therefore, she wouldn't care about her performance either. If this was the case, Raquel agreed that she wouldn't feel the pressure to practice since her recital wouldn't really matter. Because of this lack of potential threat, there would also be a lack of urgency to practice or to survive the threatening sabertooth. Unfortunately, if this was truly the case, her performance would most likely be disappointing as well, due to the lack of time spent rehearsing.

From this metaphor, Raquel understood the necessity for her body to experience some sense of urgency to avoid a disappointing performance. Using the Fight-or-Flight Awareness Checklist (Appendix 1.1), Raquel understood that no matter what physiological sensations her body objectively encountered, her subjective experience can either be productive or unproductive, depending on how she chose to perceive it. She then realized that she could channel this excessive fight-or-flight energy to motivate her to practice. As uncomfortable as the fight-or-flight alarm may be, she was able to see that this added energy could be used to her benefit rather than her detriment. As she began to understand the purpose of her body's fight-or-flight response, the shaky and sweaty fingers also began to subside. Raquel was able to apply this same principle to her actual performance during the recital. Rather than perceiving her jitters as negative anxiety, she perceived it as useful energy to liven her performance. At the end of the day, it is absolutely true that an audience would be more captivated by an energetic performance than a dull one.

Robert – 30s, Ambitious Workaholic

Robert was a young attorney in his early 30s. He described himself as a hard worker who devoted many long hours and late nights to his job in the hopes of making partner at the law firm. On top of a demanding workload that involved ensuring the accuracy of legal contracts, he was also responsible for presenting monthly reports to his superiors. Robert expressed constant knots in his stomach when working on these monthly reports. He didn't mind the day-to-day task of analyzing contracts, as tedious as they were. However, the thought of having to present delicate information to his superiors, who ultimately evaluated his partnership eligibility, gave him anxiety attacks. During these presentations, he felt as if his heart would jump out of his chest, and that he would choke on his words. Because of this and the fear of being negatively judged, he spent excessively more time perfecting the reports than necessary. Yet, this additional use of time reduced his overall productivity and distracted his attention from other areas of work.

The reality was that Robert was truly in a tough situation. On the one hand, his performance did determine whether he would make partner. On the other hand, rather than considering his overall work performance, he was giving too much weight to the evaluation of his presentations. In fact, his over-focus on these monthly reports actually reduced his general productivity. Robert needed to learn how to balance his fight-or-flight response to achieving both partnership at the firm and overall productive work output.

Robert's fight-or-flight alarm wasn't leading to procrastination ... yet. In fact, according to the fight-or-flight thermometer, his level was around an 8 with maximum energy output. However, this level of energy doesn't last forever and the body would need to recharge at some point. Unfortunately ... or fortunately for Robert, he realized this every month, right after having to give his presentation. It would take him a whole week to recover and regain his productive momentum until he ran out of energy again right after the next presentation. Now imagine if Robert continued this up-and-down cycle for several years. Where would his stamina be if he hadn't made partner yet because his overall productivity was actually lacking? Not only would he be mentally drained at this point, he would also be physically drained, which would likely result in eventual procrastination.

Robert had to slowly retrain his thinking about his anxiety attacks. Rather than judging them to depict his falsely perceived incompetence, he learned to value them as added energy to keep his momentum at optimal levels all around. To increase his awareness of his perceived experiences and resulting action, we used the Objective Sensation vs. Subjective Experience Log (Appendix 1.2) to monitor his physical sensations and emotional reactions. This helped him to constantly remind himself that "anxiety" was the subjective experience of his body's biological response to stress. And optimal levels of stress were necessary to keep him productive enough to achieve partnership at the firm. Over time, he perceived periods of increased heart rate as his body's natural signal to keep up the pace. With this in mind, he was also able to spread his energy evenly throughout his workload, which consequently increased his overall productivity.

Ted – 20yo, Perplexed Student

Ted had always been a *perfect* 4.0 student before entering college. After a rough freshman year of average grades, he began to doubt his capacity to excel academically as he was previously able to do. He described his high school years as more structured and planned. Being a college student with vague course syllabi was a completely different experience than what he was used to. He felt unprepared, had a hard time planning his readings and study schedule, and was overwhelmed by big final exams and projects. He felt assignments in high school were pre-planned; teachers simply told him what to do and when they were due. However, since his college professors were less directive, he found himself constantly anxious and paralyzed when having to make decisions as to how and when to prepare for midterms and finals.

Ted desperately wanted to excel and shine academically. However, feeling blinded by the minimal direction given by his professors, he questioned his ability to produce perfect results in his work. Consequently, he felt frustrated by the lack of structure and resorted to procrastination rather than troubleshooting the problem. This usually led to late-night cramming for tasks due the next day. Because of the heightened level of anxiety toward impending deadlines, Ted also had constant headaches and body aches, which resulted in further procrastination when he didn't feel well enough to complete his tasks. As a result, his grades were negatively impacted.

Ted's fight-or-flight triggers swung from one end of the thermometer to the other, depending upon how close his assignments were to being due. When he was intensely anxious and unable to strategize specific steps from vague syllabi, his fight-or-flight alarm stretched to a level 9. Since it's usually human nature to avoid the difficult, this resulted in procrastination. For Ted, this meant that he avoided the unfamiliar process of pre-planning for assignments that were given by his less-directive professors, because he previously didn't learn these skills in high school. He also had a hard time connecting how his perfect 4.0 high school GPA could so quickly drop to average grades in college. Again, rather than looking for the missing link to this puzzle, he resorted to procrastination, which felt safer for him than facing the threatening sabertooth.

When Ted's mindset was in avoidance mode because a deadline was distant, his fight-or-flight pendulum swung to the lower end of the thermometer. Although he still felt uneasy from knowing he was procrastinating, albeit in the back of his mind, the discomfort was less intense in the moment than having to strategize for his assignments. Since he felt blinded by the vague tasks and couldn't see the direct path to his goals, he figured he might as well keep procrastinating. However, when the threat of the sabertooth was imminent and he had limited time to meet deadlines, his energy level swung to the other direction to allow for cramming. Ted's grades continued to plummet, as did his self-confidence, while this procrastination – cramming cycle repeated.

In order for Ted to take control of this vicious sequence, he had to confront the sabertooth rather than avoid it. Ted learned to tackle the self-defeating thoughts that lowered his confidence, and to break mountainous tasks down to foreseeable steps that weren't necessarily perfect. Although this skill took much more effort to acquire, it saved him from expending even more energy procrastinating in the long run. As Ted's skills solidified, his urge to procrastinate dissipated. The fight-or-flight pendulum steadied and only swung to optimal levels when necessary. And those constant headaches and body aches were a thing of the past ... for the most part.

Julie – 45yo, Depleted Mom

Julie was a stay-at-home mom of three children. Although she made daily to-do lists of household chores, tasks, and errands, it was challenging for her to complete even 20 percent of them. Like many parents, she expressed being physically tired and sleep-deprived with little time for herself. The timeframe to complete her to-do list was usually confined to 9 a.m. to 2 p.m. when her 8- and 12-year-olds were at school. Even so, it was difficult to get things done around the house during these five hours unless her 3-year-old was napping. During these short free-time periods, she was often too exhausted and fell asleep with the toddler. At other times, she felt unmotivated to complete a task, and would say to herself, "it can wait." This resulted in feelings of guilt as she blamed herself for the time wasted and her lack of productivity. At the suggestion of the family doctor, Julie tried an exercise regimen to give her more energy. However, she described it as being boring and had a hard time staying on it. This upset her still further as she felt even less victorious.

Feeling worn out from parenthood is far too common. In Julie's case, it was no wonder why secondary tasks "can wait" when there were three young children's care to prioritize. Her fight-or-flight thermometer was typically low for these marginal non-threatening tasks, and focusing on the potential dangers to her kids was where most of her energy was spent. Thus, productivity wasn't necessarily her main problem. There really is only so much one can do with three children and limited time. Instead, the central problem was Julie's blaming of herself for the supposed lack of productivity. Whenever she criticized herself for tasks undone or exercise regimen neglected, she was basically wasting mental energy punishing herself. Ruminating on the negative doesn't increase anyone's desire to keep pursuing the unfulfilled. Thus, this led to more lethargy and procrastination than active drive.

After reviewing all of her to-do lists and assigning timeframes to each task, Julie discovered that her expectations of herself were quite impractical. Her lists had so many tasks that they would realistically take an additional seven to eight hours of time to complete than what was available in a given day. Alternately, she learned to prioritize chores, errands, and exercise, and scheduled them accordingly. This gave her expectations a reality check that was long overdue. Rather than viewing mundane tasks as demanding burdens, she began to feel rewarded and accomplished as items on her *scheduled* to-do lists were checked off, one after the other. Of course, this only increased her motivation to resume tackling items each day to continue feeling the sense of success.

By practicing awareness of the fight-or-flight reflex and implementing a few proactive techniques, many of my patients have learned to convert negative anxiety into positive energy that motivates them to accomplish specific goals. Whether the challenge is procrastination or ineffective productivity, this section of the book illustrated each individual's personal experiences using the tools to turn their fight-or-flight reflex into a positive force for achieving their goals. In order to experience objectivity, they have learned that anxiety is only their interpretation of the fight-or-flight response. Whether it's increased heart rate or sweating limbs, these same sensations are experienced when excitement occurs.

This awareness has helped to push them past the once-intolerable discomfort of anxiety. Whether they interpret the shortness of breath, shaky limbs, or pounding heart as anxiety or excitement is completely up to them. Their bodies do not know the difference. It is their minds that give these sensations the meaning of either threatening anxiety or exuberant excitement. One will drive them into a tornado of anxiety while the other will motivate them to push forward. Fortunately, they have learned how to make use of the fight-or-flight energy to work for them rather than against them. With this new awareness, you too can make use of your fight-or-flight energy to motivate and drive you to success. How the fight-or-flight sensations are perceived is truly in the eye of the beholder!

"How the fight-or-flight sensations are perceived
is all up to you."
–Dr. Yip

CHAPTER TWO

"There are no facts,
only interpretations."
–Friedrich Nietzsche

Jenny C. Yip, Psy.D., ABPP

Cognitive Distortions: Thinking Traps That Drive Your Procrastination

Have you ever fallen victim to such thoughts as: "It will take me forever to finish this job!" or "This task is impossible, so why bother?" If so, then you've experienced "cognitive distortions." The fight-or-flight response can actually prevent you from acting if you let it. This happens when irrational thoughts lead you to excessively worry about a project to the point where you feel overwhelmed with anxiety and incapable of proceeding. By learning to identify these thinking traps in your own thought process, you will remove their power over your irrational behaviors, and therefore, increase your productivity.

Perspective is nine-tenths of reality. By this, I mean that your experiences are predominantly subjective. A thousand people could read this book, and every single one will have a different experience of it, depending on when in their lives they read it, as well as the combination of their experiences up to that time. A businesswoman might view the tools in this book as a way to increase her productivity and stand out in her profession; a doctor might be interested in using them to reduce stress and increase wellness; and a student might be looking for the means to apply himself better in school. All of these people would read the same book, yet each would experience it very differently. If your experiences are subjective, and you generate thoughts based on your experiences, then it follows that your thoughts are also largely subjective. Having subjective thoughts means that they are brimming with fallacies; we call such fallacies "cognitive distortions" – inaccuracies in your thought patterns that you perceive as real.

There are 14 common cognitive distortions that mark irrational thinking. We all commit cognitive distortions regularly, and most of the time we are not even aware of their occurrence. However, with practice you can increase your awareness of these cognitive errors and correct them to prevent unnecessary stress.

List of Cognitive Distortions

All or Nothing (Either – Or) Thinking: You view things as a false alternative of either one extreme or another.

For example, *"I always procrastinate, so there's no point in getting started."*

Overgeneralization: You take isolated cases and use them as evidence to make wide inferences.

For example, *"Many people procrastinate and still do well, so it doesn't really matter that I do it."*

Jumping to Conclusions: (a) Mind reading - you assume the intention of others without evidence of what they're thinking. (b) Fortune telling - you arbitrarily forecast future occurrences.

For example, *"My boss thinks I'm a slacker,"* or *"Even if I put in the time, I'll still fail."*

Reverse Mind Reading: You expect others to know what you are thinking without first providing relevant information.

For example, *"I don't know why my parents make me play the violin. They should know how much I really hate practicing when I already have so much to do."*

Catastrophizing: You automatically think the worst-case scenario.

For example, *"I'll be fired unless I give this presentation perfectly.*

Magnification or Minimization: You make things out to be much bigger than they truly are, or unnecessarily diminish their significance.

> For example, *"If I don't get this presentation just perfect, I'll be the laughingstock of my group."* Or *"It really won't make a difference in my marathon training if I miss just this one day of practice."*

Mental Filter: You completely zoom in on the negative and ignore any positive.

> For example, *"I've only finished one assignment; I'll never get through the other five."*

Discounting the Positives: You disregard or trivialize the positive elements about yourself, such as your efforts, attributes, qualities, or achievements.

> For example, *"I'm no genius ... I just got lucky."*

Exceptional Rule Justification: You make judgments that only apply to specific cases, and you do not really believe it at other times, for other circumstances, or with other people.

> For example, *"If I watch a little TV now and pull an all-nighter to finish this paper, I would still meet the morning deadline and wouldn't really be procrastinating."*

Irrelevant Connection: You link two hypotheses that are unrelated.

> For example, *"It's okay to procrastinate a little on this proposal for now, because I am too distracted with emails at the moment."*

Emotional Reasoning: You rationalize based on how you feel rather than objective reality.

For example, *"I'm feeling too tired to work on this project, so it's best that I put it off until I feel more energetic to produce amazing results."*

Labeling: You assign negative descriptors rather than describing specific behaviors.

For example, *"I still haven't started my project; I'm a failure."*

Personalization and Blame: You hold yourself or other people personally responsible for things that aren't entirely within anyone's control.

For example, *"Because Sheila distracted me, I haven't finished any of my work!"*

"Should" Statements: You criticize yourself, others, inanimate objects, or uncontrollable situations with "shoulds" or "shouldn'ts."

For example, *"I should have finished this earlier."*

As you can see, cognitive distortions lead to unrealistic negative thoughts. Such thoughts trigger unnecessary anxiety, which often prevents you from proceeding with your work rather than motivating you. Procrastinating will result in further irrational negative thoughts if you let it. Before you realize it, the vicious procrastination cycle has begun.

THOUGHTS
"I always procrastinate."

BEHAVIORS
Procrastination

EMOTIONS
Anxious, Overwhelmed

If you say, "I always procrastinate," then it seems reasonable for you to conclude that "I might as well wait until the last minute again." This would then cause you to feel anxious and overwhelmed, triggering additional procrastination. Consequently, your recurrent procrastination further reinforces your negative thought pattern, resulting in your continual procrastination on future projects. However, by recognizing your cognitive distortions (*all-or-nothing thinking* and *fortune-telling*), you can interrupt the vicious cycle and put a stop to it. For example, you could instead say, "I usually procrastinate, and because of that, I end up rushing at the last minute. This time I'll try starting earlier and see how that works out."

Procrastination feeds off a vicious cycle: Irrational thoughts lead to irrational emotions, which then result in irrational actions. By breaking this cycle of distorted thoughts, you will become more capable of making quality decisions and addressing the consequences of previous poor decisions. For example, instead of ruminating over the fact that you have been procrastinating and feeding off the negative fight-or-flight experience, you can become proactive and get started on your work by putting that fight-or-flight energy to action.

How do you learn to recognize cognitive distortions if they are weaved so intricately into seemingly realistic thoughts? Recognizing and correcting these thinking traps will take time and practice. As you start, you may only notice one here or there. With time, though, you will learn to adjust them almost without thinking about it. How do you start? Whenever you find yourself procrastinating or feeling overly anxious from an excessive fight-or-flight experience, take it as a red flag that you need to begin checking your thoughts for distortions. There is never a rational reason to be procrastinating, so irrational thoughts are the likely culprit. You may, for example, be thinking, "I am a procrastinator, so I will put this off until the last minute." Once you recognize your thought, ask yourself, "Is this absolutely true? Are there any other explanations for this? Where is the evidence? Am I being trapped by one or more cognitive distortions?" If you look hard, you might see that you are both *labeling* yourself as a procrastinator and, as a result, *fortune-telling* that you will procrastinate.

Now that you have recognized your fallacies, correct them. Rephrase your previous thought in a way that removes the irrationalities. For example, you could adjust your thought to, "In the past I have procrastinated, which has caused me to produce poor quality work at the last minute." This is a fact-based statement demonstrating cause and effect. Once you are viewing your experiences free from distortion, you can make a more effective judgment of how to proceed. If procrastinating has led you to finish at the last minute in the past, then this time you could try starting early and see what happens. Next, we'll look at some tools that you can use to overcome procrastination once you recognize its presence.

PERSONAL ANECDOTES

Raquel – 12yo, Piano Prodigy

It took Raquel some time to understand how the human mind could be so frequently invaded by cognitive distortions. At only 12 years old, she had limited life experience and a young, still developing mind. As such, a lot of time had to be spent educating her about how thoughts were based on perception, and perception was shaped by our personal biases rather than factual reality. Raquel learned that the brain had to filter out much of the sensory information it took in. This was how the brain maintained efficiency, albeit at the expense of accuracy. Consequently there was a lot of information that her brain processed that was also out of her awareness. This is essentially where the phrase, "perspective is 9/10 of reality" comes from.

To help Raquel relate to this, I asked her to imagine watching a movie with 10 of her friends, and whether each person would have the exact same viewpoint. Of course, similar to the many variations of eye witness testimonies, each observer would see a different angle of the same situation. How they perceived the event would depend on many factors, such as their mood in that moment, the amount of sleep they had, the position from where they witnessed the event, who they were with, whether they identified with the people in the event, and so on and so forth. We applied this notion to her irrational drive to perform perfectly, illustrating the point that what may seem perfect to one person may be imperfect to another. This was why people have disagreements. Blame it on personal biases and perspectives. She quickly understood the point.

Once Raquel was able to make the connection between biases and thoughts, our next goal was to determine the negative thinking patterns that trapped her in procrastination mode, using the Cognitive Distortion

Thought Record (Appendices 2.1 & 2.2). After some probing, we identified that she tended to *catastrophize*, *jump to conclusions*, *magnify*, and *discount the positives* whenever the threat of a recital loomed near. She generally had thoughts such as, "I won't be able to play perfectly because this piece of music is much more difficult than the last," "Everyone will be focused on me and see every mistake I make," and "I'll mess up and people will laugh at me." She had a hard time taking her skills, efforts, and previous recital experiences into consideration when judging her next performance. She also realized the conundrum that if the audience didn't care about her performance, then she wouldn't bother to practice and would likely perform even worse. Raquel wasn't willing to give up piano altogether, and was essentially stuck in a "damned if you do; damned if you don't" scenario.

To help her move in one direction or another and really make obvious the wiser path to take, we listed the pros and cons of each option. After a thorough analysis of the two lists, she chose to utilize the time available to her for rehearsing rather than ruminating on faulty thinking errors. This was achieved by identifying and disputing the mind traps whenever she felt anxious from the urge to procrastinate. Over time, Raquel became adept at taking evidence into consideration based on her skills and past performances rather than her biased perceptions.

Robert – 30s, Ambitious Workaholic

When cognitive distortions were explained to Robert, his initial response was outrage. He prided himself for skills in logical reasoning that he believed were part of every attorney's training, and denied falling victim to such thinking fallacies. I took advantage of his enjoyment of philosophy to steer his attention toward his own lack of intellectual humility, which was central to rational dialectics. In fact, his absolute determination that he would never commit a thinking error was in itself an *all or nothing* distortion. Once he realized this, he was immediately embarrassed and proceeded to call himself all sorts of names such as "idiot," "moron," and "fool," to name just a few. To this, I highlighted his next thinking trap: *labeling*. However, Robert brought up an interesting point: Why was it a cognitive distortion to label?

I explained that whenever we label, it is a mental shortcut, a scapegoat accusation and the easy way out. Rather than taking the time and mental effort to examine the evidence for such a label, we simply attribute a random term to a person, object, or situation without thinking further about it. This is basically one of the main conundrums the human brain faces: efficiency vs. accuracy. To efficiently process simultaneous information quickly, accuracy would be lost. Yet, accuracy often requires painstaking time to achieve. Thus, when Robert *labeled*, he didn't conscientiously analyze the accuracy of the name-calling. Plus, assigning labels is generally unproductive since labels don't give any detail about the reasoning behind them. It would've been much more effective for Robert to simply and accurately indicate that he felt foolish because he didn't consider the possibility of making such thinking fallacies.

Once Robert was on board that he, too, did commit many cognitive distortions that flew under the radar, we were able to look deeper at specific thoughts that kept him from optimal productivity. He identified the following key thinking patterns: "If I'm anxious, it means I lack confidence and am incompetent." *(Irrelevant connection)* "They will see my uneasiness and think I'm unqualified to make partner." *(Jumping to conclusions)* "I should spend more time on monthly reports to lessen my nerves when presenting them." *(Should statement)* Because of this mental sequence, Robert spent excessively more time perfecting the reports at the expense of his overall productive output. To determine the accuracy of this rationale, we turned each statement into a question. "If I'm anxious, does it truly mean that I lack confidence and am incompetent?" "Are there any other reasons for feeling anxious unrelated to confidence and competency?" Obviously, there were many reasons for anxiety that had nothing to do with confidence or competency.

Through this process, what Robert realized was that no matter how much time he spent preparing reports, he was still having a rough time presenting them. The problem was inherent in his fear of being negatively evaluated, which would hinder his chances of making partner at the firm. Yet, the drop in his overall productivity also hindered his goal to become partner. At this point, Robert realized that the logical step was to spread his energy evenly across his workload, rather than digging further into a lose-lose situation. As his productivity level rose, he felt more hopeful about his chances at partnership. This, in turn, helped him to further tackle thinking traps surrounding his fear of incompetency. Over time, Robert was able to identify the cognitive distortions as they occurred, and correct them so his thinking reflected reality more accurately.

Ted – 20yo, Perplexed Student

To tackle cognitive distortions, you have to first catch them. This was Ted's biggest challenge. He constantly felt a nagging sense of uneasiness, yet couldn't place where it stemmed from. He felt apprehensive even during activities that he would ordinarily take pleasure in. In addition, the constant anxiety was so extensive that it often led to headaches and body aches, which puzzled him even further. I explained to Ted that thinking errors were difficult to capture because they fly beneath the level of conscious awareness most of the time. Even people who were well-trained in logical thinking or cognitive distortions still made such errors. Unfortunately, life in the real world eliminated the luxury of having sufficient time for accuracy in distortion-free thinking. Nevertheless, this didn't mean that we couldn't minimize these thinking traps as much as possible.

Although Ted was often frustrated that he couldn't perfectly tackle all cognitive distortions that inundated his mind, he learned that an effective method to increase his awareness of them was to use his fight-or-flight response as a red flag. Whenever he experienced a negative emotion, such as uneasiness or apprehension, that was his body's natural alarm signaling danger – real or imagined. Whenever he felt this disturbance, he had to determine whether it was an actual sabertooth threat or a false alarm based on his biased perception. If the anxiety did indeed stem from a false alarm, then cognitive distortions were the culprit.

As Ted's awareness increased, he realized that his mind was frequently trapped in thinking errors, especially when he procrastinated. Unfortunately, this was almost always the case, which was what kept him on constant edge. Whenever he stressed over trying to perfect his academic assignments and did nothing about them, he would still ruminate over them. Even when he wasn't conscientiously thinking about schoolwork, his mind was trapped in negative thoughts.

Some of his thoughts included: "I'm feeling too achy to do perfect work now. It can wait." *(Emotional Reasoning)* "There's absolutely no hope getting my GPA up. I've become a failure." *(All or Nothing, Labeling)* "There's no point worrying about it now because I'm clueless right this second." *(Minimization, Irrelevant Connection)* "It's not really procrastinating if I still get the work done and turned in on time, even if it's at the last minute." *(Exceptional Rule Justification)* While Ted still had many thinking errors, he was more aware of them and became more accountable for his actions because of them. Whenever he felt an irritating emotion, he would seek out the thinking trap that triggered it. Once he determined the contributing thoughts, he would ask himself whether they were honestly true. If not, which was usually the case, he would correct for the faulty thoughts and prevent them from affecting his actions.

Julie – 45yo, Depleted Mom

In order for Julie to maintain her motivation to tackle her daily errands and chores, it was crucial for her to feel rewarded for tasks accomplished rather than punished for those that were incomplete. I explained to Julie that feelings of reward and punishment stemmed from her thoughts and determined her reactions. In other words, thoughts led to emotions that shaped behaviors. In Julie's case, whenever she felt unmotivated, it was due to her irrational thoughts (self-blame) that led to her irrational emotions (guilt), which then resulted in her irrational actions (avoidance). By accomplishing her goals, she felt a sense of reward and success, which then reinforced the behaviors that produced these positive results. On the other hand, feeling punished from failure to achieve her goals led to further avoidance of the undesirable emotion.

In reality, nobody would want to feel terrible. However, unless those cognitive distortions that caused the unproductive sequence were caught, Julie's avoidance behaviors would trigger further negative thoughts. Ultimately, this thinking trap would feed off a vicious cycle of overall unproductivity, which was exactly what happened. Fortunately, Julie had an easier time identifying the thinking errors that were committed because of the negative emotions she felt from self-blame and criticisms. She found herself having thoughts such as: "I've done it again and wasted time napping when I should've been cleaning up." *(Personalization and Blame; Should Statement)* "I'm such a slowpoke; I've only gotten one chore done." *(Labeling; Mental Filter)* "I've failed to exercise again just like I've failed in so many other things in life." *(Overgeneralization; Personalization and Blame)*

As Julie became more and more aware of these thought traps, she realized that her motivation to tackle tasks decreased as the negative thoughts increased. Using a thought record (Appendix 2.2), she spent much time training herself to either look for evidence that supported her thoughts or develop alternative thoughts that reflected reality more accurately. As she

33

discovered that her expectations were unreasonable, she was able to assess and plan for her days more accordingly. Consequently, Julie felt less negative about herself, while she responded to her chores and errands realistically and productively.

When I first introduce the list of cognitive distortions, many of my patients react with, "I don't do any of these." Naturally so, people don't walk around all day with these thoughts at the forefront of their attention. However, cognitive distortions simply serve to reinforce the cycle of procrastination. The thought traps not only prevented these individuals from completing tasks, they produced extra anxiety that consumed their mental capacity and delayed task completion even further.

After accepting that such negative thoughts exist and taking time to recognize their thinking patterns, each of these individuals has learned to prevent procrastination by adjusting for those irrationalities. They have learned to identify cognitive distortions by monitoring their thoughts in a small notebook or digital notepad that is available wherever they go. They write down negative thoughts whenever they notice it, and use the thought record to determine the validity of each thought at a more convenient time. They have learned to challenge each recorded thought by questioning it, and if there is no evidence, then they write down a corrected form of the thought. To more easily identify thinking fallacies, they use the fight-or-flight response as a signal that a thought – positive or negative – has just occurred.

Similar to these personal accounts, unless you have taken a course on logic and mental fallacies, or have had training in cognitive behavioral therapy (CBT), you may also have little awareness of the cognitive distortions that run wild in your mind. Although some people may be embarrassed to admit they are prone to such irrational thoughts, the reality is that everyone commits such fallacies many, many times a day, simply because the brain often values efficiency over accuracy. Now that you have this knowledge, you too can use the list of cognitive distortions to identify fallacies in your thinking patterns, and put a stop to procrastination. The first step to any focused change is awareness of those erroneous interpretations, as well as intellectual humility – acceptance that an alternative view exists.

SECTION II

"Let our advance worrying
become advance thinking and planning."
–Winston Churchill

Creating Your Personal Action Plan

You may have noticed a common theme throughout this book: It is easy to procrastinate; it is difficult to succeed. Wouldn't it be easier to just put this task off until tomorrow? Wouldn't it be easier to ignore cognitive distortions than to spend time correcting them? It most certainly might be. You didn't come here to take the easy path though; you came here to learn how to succeed. So far, we've looked at reasons why we all procrastinate and how to avoid these barriers. Now we will look at specific tools and strategies that will help you overcome procrastination directly.

CHAPTER THREE

"The man who removes a mountain
begins by carrying away small stones."
(Chinese Proverb)

Breaking Mountains into Molehills

The first tool for overcoming procrastination is to break mountains into molehills. Perhaps the largest contributor to procrastination is that you have trouble seeing the end result of your work. If I asked you to write a novel right now, would you be able to? No? Why not? Writing an entire novel is an overwhelmingly large task. It takes some authors months, even years, to complete one. If you sit down and say, "Today I am going to write a novel," it is simply not going to happen. The task is too complex and your approach too vague. What if, instead, I asked you to come up with a basic plot for a novel today? You could probably think of hundreds. A man searches for his long lost brother. A police-woman hunts down a dangerous vigilante. Suddenly, your novel has direction. Writing an entire novel may be overwhelming, yet it seems relatively simple to think up a plot or a protagonist.

Another way to think about it is this: Imagine that you are running a marathon, a 26.2-mile run. You are standing at the starting line. Can you see the finish line from your position? Of course not. As with many tasks, your end goal is farther than you can see. However, can you see 100 yards away? Unless visually impaired, the answer is probably yes! So run those 100 yards. When you reach the end of that, how far can you see? Another 100 yards? Alright, run those 100 yards as well. Even though you can't see the finish line until you reach it, you can see smaller goals that you know you can accomplish.

These two examples introduce the basic concept of breaking mountains into molehills. Whenever you are having trouble working on a task, you are likely overwhelmed by how difficult it appears. However, by breaking the task down into smaller, easily achievable goals, you gain confidence as a result of recognizing that you can complete the task. When your plan for approaching a task is vague, it makes the task appear insurmountable, no matter how simple it might seem. In fact, if you don't plan out your goals, they become far more difficult, even impossible, to achieve. Planning your goals simply means breaking them down task by task, and making each task simple enough to achieve without feeling bogged down or overburdened.

I recently went rock climbing in Alaska. I needed to climb a total of three steep rock faces. For the first two, I planned my approach and was able to complete them fairly easily. "That wasn't so bad," I thought. Distracted by my overconfidence, I began to climb the third rock face without first judging the situation. About halfway into my climb, I came across a large overhang, and was unable to get past it. Had I planned my ascent before I began climbing, I would have foreseen such an obstacle and already had in mind ways to overcome it. The same is true of any task. If you simply start working with no plan, then when you come to an obstacle, you are going to have no plan of attack and will become easily overwhelmed. By breaking mountains into molehills, you can turn complex, challenging goals into simple, easily conquerable steps.

Whether you have long-term goals such as becoming a partner at a law firm or short-term goals like writing that paper due next week, strategize your roadmap by planning backward. Start with your desired goal and determine each successive step sequentially, including the associated timeframes needed for each step, until you reach the most immediate action. Doing so will help you establish the most efficient route and see potential obstacles along the way. This will save you a lot of time and headache in the long run.

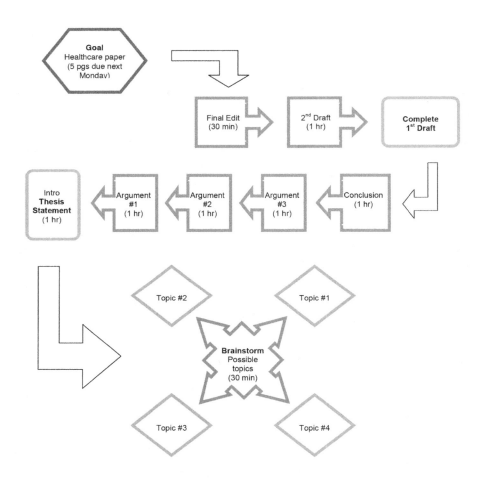

To explain this process, let's look at a common task that involves breaking mountains into molehills: writing a paper. Have you ever tried to write a paper by simply sitting down at a keyboard and typing? It is incredibly difficult. Again, this is because the task is too vague. In primary and secondary school, you are taught a series of tools that help you push past this. The first step is to brainstorm and come up with a series of possible topics and subtopics to include. During brainstorming, you also develop your thesis, the main argument in your paper. Writing a paper is impossible if you do not have direction or focus. By brainstorming, you determine in which direction you would like to take your paper.

Now, instead of writing a paper about healthcare reform, you have an argument, such as "healthcare reform needs to focus primarily on the role of insurance companies, since healthcare costs have skyrocketed for consumers, while healthcare providers haven't benefited from this price increase." You also build ideas about how to argue your point, such as referencing the history of various insurance companies and their profit margins over time.

Once you have determined an overall direction for your paper, you need to make an outline for it. An outline truly breaks the paper into molehills by laying out a specific course of action that involves easily achievable, individual tasks. When you outline your paper, you will decide how many paragraphs you would like and what the topic of each paragraph will be. For example, the outline for your healthcare reform paper might include the following:

A) Introduction (1 – 2 paragraphs)
  1. Explain topic and why it's important.
  2. Thesis statement.
B) History of Insurance Companies
  1. Existence of various companies (1 – 2 paragraphs)
  2. Patient Premiums (2 – 3 paragraphs)
    a. Profit margins from raising premiums.
    b. Past premium hikes.
C) Current Trend in Healthcare Insurance
  1. Consumer (3 – 4 paragraphs)
    a. Ever increasing premiums.
    b. Low rate of reimbursement.
    c. High deductibles.
    d. High annual out of pocket expense.
    e. Certain brand medications not covered.

    2. Providers (4 – 5 paragraphs)
        a. Low negotiated rates of reimbursement.
        b. Increase rates of services to compensate for difference.
            i. Increased rates are assumed by consumers if insurance doesn't cover.
        c. Highly sought-after professionals with specific specialties are leaving insurance panels due to low rates of reimbursement.
            i. Consumers must go out of network in order to obtain quality healthcare for specific conditions that are not covered or are minimally covered by insurance plans.
D) Conclusion
    1. Restate main argument. (1 paragraph)
    2. Suggest new policies. (2 – 3 paragraphs)
        a. Maximum allowances of profit margins that insurance companies can gain over time in order for consumers to afford quality healthcare.

Now that you have finished your outline, your paper has a very specific focus and path, and you have broken it into easily achievable tasks. Do you feel you could write this whole paper right now? Maybe not. However, do you think that you could write the introductory paragraph? Sure you do! That seems pretty easy. How long do you think it might take you? An hour, or maybe two? Then set aside an hour or so each night for the next five nights, and your paper will be finished!

You now have at your disposal the first tool for conquering procrastination: breaking mountains into molehills. You have probably written a paper before, and you may even say to yourself, "I've used outlines in the past, but they still don't keep me from procrastinating." This is an excellent point. You have the outline ... now what? It's time to learn the second tool you will need to stop procrastination: scheduling.

PERSONAL ANECDOTES

Raquel – 12yo, Piano Prodigy

While breaking mountains into molehills wasn't Raquel's central problem, she was able to benefit from this tool, especially during the week leading up to each recital. During this period, she tended to procrastinate practicing her music due to irrational fears of performing poorly. Although she learned to utilize her fight-or-flight energy productively and was effectively turning around thought traps, she still felt somewhat overwhelmed, and rightly so. In Raquel's words, it was "all work and no fun."

To lighten this pressure, we broke down the work and incorporated some fun. Raquel chose various songs that she enjoyed playing. After every 40 minutes of practicing for her recital, she spent 20 minutes playing these other songs. We further broke down this 20-minute free-play time to include previous recital pieces that she now enjoyed. Playing previously performed songs reminded her of past successful recitals and the skills she actually acquired. Thus, rather than her typical pressured rehearsal schedule, each practice cycle followed this pattern:

40 minutes – Recital practice
20 minutes – Free-play
     - 1 previous recital song
     - Any enjoyable song

This newly created schedule – incorporating free-play periods that Raquel found rewarding – alleviated some of the stress she experienced. Nevertheless, I reminded her that the fight-or-flight energy that was triggered from upcoming recitals was necessary for success. Without it, she wouldn't feel the urgency to react and overcome challenges. In fact, if we were all too complacent, then there wouldn't be anything to motivate us.

As such, there also wouldn't be much progression in life. Raquel had to accept the reality that she would continue to feel some tension whenever recitals came up, which was necessary to energize her to practice and perform well. However, it didn't have to be all work and no fun either.

Robert – 30s, Ambitious Workaholic

Robert's main goal was to make partner at the law firm. Yet, he didn't have a plan of attack and hadn't strategized how this goal would be accomplished. Instead, he aimlessly devoted many long hours to his job, hoping that would show his commitment to the firm and be enough to make partner. I shared with Robert that a goal without a plan was just an empty wish. What he desperately needed was a roadmap depicting exactly what he had to do to get to where he wanted to be. Using the Clarification Map (Appendix 3.1), we planned backward from the end goal of achieving partnership. In order to reach the goal, he had to excel in three main areas: accurately preparing and executing legal contracts, analyzing and presenting monthly financial reports, and bringing a minimum of x number of clients to the firm.

The most challenging area for Robert was determining how to spread a reasonable amount of time across all three domains to yield the most effective results – without burning out. This meant spending less time on monthly reports, and more time executing legal contracts and generating more clients. Once Robert learned to maximize his fight-or-flight alarm and escape from thought traps, he was able to spread his energy more evenly between reports and contracts. However, he didn't give any thought to how he would build his client base. After some contemplation, Robert established several strategies to achieve this sub-goal, including networking with colleagues from other firms and professions that could utilize his services, and taking his bigger accounts out to lunch/dinner or sporting events to generate client referrals.

Robert made a list of colleagues and clients that he would touch base with in the next 30 days, and spent the newly allotted "building clients" time making calls to connect with them. At the end of each month, he evaluated his progress and repeated this procedure, which kept him on track toward the goals. Without this clarification map, Robert wandered aimlessly in the dark without sight of reaching the end of the tunnel. Through this process, he was able to check back on each sub-goal, determine the effectiveness of his approach, and re-strategize if necessary to remain on a productive path.

Ted – 20yo, Perplexed Student

Overall, Ted had a difficult time preparing assignments from course syllabi. His previous method was to sit for extensively long hours to fully finish an assignment to perfection. This was tremendously stressful and usually left him in procrastination mode. Ted wasn't familiar with the approach of planning backward from task completion to each sequential step. Because of the lack of a foreseeable map, as well as a drop in GPA, he repeatedly warned himself that he was no longer the perfect student he once was in high school. This constant reminder raised his anxiety level whenever he attempted to approach an assignment, and in turn, paralyzed and led him to further procrastinate. In essence, Ted was spinning in circles rather than moving in a specified direction. He needed to learn how to break down vague, mountainous assignments into smaller, measurable steps.

For an upcoming presentation, we used the Stepwise Goal Planner (Appendix 3.2) – a more thorough worksheet that helped him gain effective planning skills. After reviewing his syllabus and some deliberation, Ted decided that there were three parts to giving the presentation: writing the speech, preparing the PowerPoint, and memorizing the main points to talk about. He broke each of these sub-goals further into specific tasks and estimated timeframes required to complete each step.

1) Writing Speech (8 hours total)
   • Brainstorm topics – 30 minutes
   • Research literature – 1 hour
   • Review literature – 1 hour
   • Prepare outline – 30 minutes
   • Write intro – 1 hour
   • Write supporting points – 2 hours
   • Write conclusion – 1 hour
   • Edit draft – 1 hour

2) PowerPoint (1 hour total)
   • Select template and format – 5 minutes
   • Copy and paste main points – 30 minutes
   • Edit and format – 25 minutes

3) Memorization (2.5 hours total)
   • Rehearse intro – 30 minutes
   • Rehearse supporting points – 30 minutes
   • Rehearse conclusion – 30 minutes
   • Final practice with PowerPoint – 1 hour

Breaking the vague assignment of giving an hour-long presentation into these measurable steps provided Ted a formulated roadmap. Because he was able to see each successive target, he had a direction to proceed toward and was no longer paralyzed by the unknown. Rather than blindly starting tasks without a plan or trying to complete projects singlehandedly, both which left him in procrastination mode, I instructed Ted to use this approach whenever he felt overwhelmed by assignments. Once he became efficient at breaking mountains into molehills, he was able to timely map out even the most vague, difficult projects. The quality of his work was also much improved from the days of last-minute cramming.

Julie – 45yo, Depleted Mom

One of Julie's most difficult tasks to accomplish was getting into an exercise regimen. Like many people, she would join the gym as part of a resolution to get in shape and increase energy levels. However, whenever she missed a scheduled workout, it would be easy for her to miss another. Sooner or later, she was off the wagon completely. Each time she fell off the wagon, her motivation to resume dwindled. The reality was that Julie had no idea where or how to start a healthy, effective exercise regimen. She wasn't able to consistently implement exercise routines before having her first child. Now with three young children, the attempts were even more fruitless. Plus, she placed so much emphasis on "working out" that the whole notion became overwhelmingly laborious.

What Julie needed was a plan of action that consisted of two main criteria: a) to find fulfilling activities that would also get the "workout" job done; and b) to break down activities so they were realistic and manageable within her free time. Since it wasn't practical for her to get to a gym with her very limited spare time, the idea of rejoining a gym was scratched completely. After some brainstorming, Julie came up with a list of activities that she might enjoy more than her treadmill at home. I instructed her to try each activity at least three times to truly give each a fair chance, then choose two to four activities. Through the process of elimination, she settled on:

1) Brisk walking with her 3-year-old in the stroller at a nearby park.
2) Yoga at home provided by an online website, or at a studio that was within a five-minute walking distance.
3) Dance via DVD at home.

We took each of these activities and broke them down to ensure that the new routine would be feasible and manageable. There were two sub-goals: a) engage in any one of the three exercises three to five times weekly; b) exercise 30 to 60 minutes each time. This gave Julie the flexibility to exercise even on days with less free time, or miss certain days altogether without condemning her to feelings of guilt and discouragement. Since the idea of working out for 60 minutes was daunting, we strategized the following plan to slowly reach the target:

Week 1: 20 minutes - brisk walking, yoga, or dance
Week 2: 30 minutes - brisk walking, yoga, or dance
Week 3: 40 minutes - brisk walking, yoga, or dance
Week 4: 50 minutes - brisk walking, yoga, or dance
Week 5: 60 minutes - brisk walking, yoga, or dance

For Julie, setting a workout goal without any planning was no different than walking an unfamiliar maze blindfolded. Her attempts were unproductive, and the lack of success contributed to unnecessary self-blame. After breaking the mountain of exercise into molehills, she had a path and specific targets that guided her endeavor. This helped her to not only successfully implement an exercise regimen; it was one she could stick to and feel rewarded by.

As with each of these individuals' experiences, breaking ambiguous tasks into smaller, measurable targets may initially seem like added work. So is procrastination. The dangers of working with vague mountainous tasks without clear, distinct goals are numerous. Having no plan of attack, losing focus, getting sidetracked, having no plan B when obstacles occur, believing the objective is impossible, feeling overwhelmed, and procrastinating are just a few possible consequences.

Similar to any skill worth attaining, the ability to innately and easily break mountains into molehills comes with practice. As the skill becomes familiar, it develops into a natural habit. As each individual has learned, it is more efficient to take the time to make goals precise and easily reachable than to jump into a task blindfolded. By breaking mountains into molehills, each person has minimized the anxiety and torture from procrastination in order to maximize their productive efforts. So can you! What else have you got to lose except more time for procrastinating?

CHAPTER FOUR

"He who fails to plan,
plans to fail."
(Italian Proverb)

Scheduling for Accountability

The next tool for overcoming procrastination is to actually plan the completion of each molehill. I do not simply mean that you need to "plan" to do them – you do that already! I mean that, once you have broken the mountain into molehills, you must take each hill and plan a specific date and time of when you will complete the task using a scheduler or planner.

This is vital because, as we have discussed, you already think "there is always tomorrow." If you do not mark a specific time and date when you will accomplish your task, then you are not held accountable when you fail to complete it. Once you place it in the planner, it becomes a deadline that you must meet. A "to-do list" does not count as planning, because even if you have it listed, you do not have a specific time to accomplish it. In a 24-four hour period, there are countless opportunities to procrastinate, and that to-do list will just get longer and longer if you let it.

Suppose that you plan to clean your house on Saturday. You wake up in the morning and say, "First I need to eat breakfast, exercise, and shower. Cleaning can wait until I do those things." Then, at noon you might say, "Well, it's lunch time now. After I eat, I'll work on it." Lunch might leave you wanting some downtime to relax. After taking a break, the clock is inching toward late afternoon. "Oh, I forgot that I need to get groceries and go to the bank before it closes! I'll start cleaning when I get back." By the time you return home, it's five or six in the evening. "I'm hungry from all these errands I've been running. I guess it couldn't hurt to eat before I clean. Otherwise I just won't have the energy to focus anyway." In another hour, you've finished eating your dinner. "It's late now and I'm tired. I think I'll just take it easy the rest of the night, or maybe go out with some friends. I can clean the house tomorrow." Suddenly, an entire day has gone by, and you've made little or no progress toward accomplishing your goal.

Now imagine instead that you had broken down cleaning your house and planned it into your schedule:

7:45 a.m. – 9:00 a.m.:   Jog, shower, breakfast
9:00 a.m. – 10:15 a.m.:   Clean kitchen
- Clean stove
- Wipe counters
- Unload dishwasher
- Mop floor

10:15 a.m. – 12:00 p.m.: Clean living room and bedrooms
- Wash clothes and sheets
- Tidy up random items
- Dust
- Vacuum

12:00 p.m. – 2:00 p.m.: Eat lunch; groceries and bank

All of these tasks seem easily manageable within the given time limits. Of course, you would have to adjust the timeframe according to how much you need to clean. Even if it took you three hours to clean your place, you are done by noon. Plus, you've gotten your breakfast and exercise in as well. You've also written in your grocery shopping and bank run, so you won't forget and have to do those at the last minute. If it takes you until 2 p.m. to do all of these things, you still have the whole afternoon ahead of you to relax, go out with friends, or whatever your heart desires.

Scheduling tasks commits you to doing them. A good analogy is a doctor's appointment. If you wake up Monday morning and have a doctor's appointment, you are committed to going to that appointment. It doesn't matter if you don't feel like going or have other things you would rather do, you need to go and are going to go. Why? Because it's scheduled. You've made a commitment to your doctor and to your physical health to get checked up at that time. Scheduling tasks functions in exactly the same way. When you schedule it, you're telling yourself that it will be done at that time.

Certainly, just because you have scheduled something does not mean that it is set in stone. Each day of our lives is full of unexpected turns, and as such, it is important to make your schedule flexible. What if that Saturday morning, for example, your friend locked her keys in her car and needed you to bring her a spare set? Your friend's situation seems more pressing than cleaning your house, so you would likely choose to help her. In such situations, you must use your own judgment to determine whether your schedule can be rearranged. If instead of merely cleaning your house, you were preparing for a presentation that you needed to give at noon and it would take more than a few hours to help your friend, then you would probably send your apologies to your friend, ask her to call AAA, and get back to work. Only you can judge the importance of your scheduled tasks relative to new situations that may arise.

If you do decide to put off your scheduled assignments, it is vital that you reschedule them to a specific time and date immediately. Perhaps your friend calls for help after you have already cleaned your kitchen. You can reschedule cleaning your living room and bedroom for the same time Sunday morning, and ask your friend to come with you to the grocery store and bank when you pick her up today. If you do not reschedule your tasks to a specific time and date, you will once again find yourself caught in the endless cycle of procrastination. So if you really want to succeed at being more productive, then do yourself a favor and make sure all your tasks are scheduled – even the daily mundane ones.

PERSONAL ANECDOTES

Raquel – 12yo, Piano Prodigy

Scheduling was really useful for Raquel and not only for piano rehearsals either. She was able to benefit from having a planner for all her school-work as well. She also learned to gauge the amount of time needed for specific tasks simply by practicing the art of scheduling. Although Raquel already had a student planner that was provided by her school, it wasn't detailed enough for efficient scheduling. Her school planner simply had sections of lines for filling in assignments. It got messy and unreadable when deadlines needed to be adjusted, and it was difficult to tell when assignments were due or had to be done unless you turned to that page to look for it. Raquel needed a detailed planner (Appendix 4.2) with daily hours broken down into 15-minute increments. I instructed her to write with pencil so items could be easily erased and moved, and to use a paper-clip to bookmark the current day for quick navigation.

During the weekdays, Raquel typically allotted 3-6 p.m. for homework and 6-7 p.m. for piano practice. I instructed her to break each day's assignments down to fit into the three-hour time span. She had to gauge how much time she needed and could not go over the three hours. When it came time to begin her first assignment, she had to finish it within the time she estimated. Whenever this time was up, she had to stop the task and begin the next assignment. This procedure continued until she reached the end of the allotted time for the last assignment. If there were any tasks uncompleted, she had to schedule them accordingly and recycle the same process until all assignments were complete. For instance:

Original Schedule
3:00 – 3:30 p.m.: Math - pages 67-69, odd numbers
3:30 – 4:15 p.m.: English - read chapters 12 & 13

4:15 – 5:00 p.m.: Science - page 109, questions 2-5
5:00 – 6:00 p.m.: Break
6:00 – 6:40 p.m.: Piano recital practice
6:40 – 7:00 p.m.: Piano free-play

Schedule Addendum 1
5:05 – 5:20 p.m.: Math - page 69, odd numbers
5:20 – 5:40 p.m.: Science - questions 4 & 5
5:40 – 6:00 p.m.: Break

Schedule Addendum 2
5:40 – 5:45 p.m.: Science - finish question 5
5:45 – 6:00 p.m.: Break

By estimating and timing her assignments, Raquel learned to establish a realistic schedule and completed her work in a timely manner. Before utilizing this approach, she would spend an inordinate amount of time on homework. She would get overwhelmed by the seemingly never-ending tasks, lose focus, and engage in something unrelated to the task at hand. Incomplete homework would then run into time reserved for piano lessons, which gave an excuse to skip practice altogether. Timing and scheduling her assignments and piano rehearsals kept her on track both academically and for recitals. Plus, she felt less anxious since she saw an end to each task. She even made a game out of this strategy – rewarding herself with a small treat whenever she was able to beat her own time.

Robert – 30s, Ambitious Workaholic

Scheduling was not an unfamiliar practice for Robert. Being an attorney, he was used to making daily appointments with clients or for meetings. However, he had trouble finding time for networking to build his client base. He spent most of his work hours analyzing contracts and preparing monthly reports. Although he was aware by this point that he needed to bring more clients to the firm in order to make partner, he felt there wasn't enough time with all of his responsibilities. While he made a list of colleagues and clients to contact and connect with over a month ago, he hadn't communicated with anyone from the list.

To illustrate that there were enough hours in a week for networking – 168 to be exact – we broke down what a typical schedule looked like. If Robert worked 12 hours a day at five days a week, that would be a 60-hour work week. Then we allocated 7 hours a night for sleep, and 4 hours a day for personal hygiene, eating, traveling, exercise, and other miscellaneous necessities. At seven days a week, that added another 77 hours to the week for a total of 137 committed hours. This still left him with 31 hours per week of unscheduled time. However, the goal wasn't to increase Robert's work hours with networking obligations. Even if he took people out for meals, it used up part of the four hours already allotted to the day and wouldn't really be taking too much more time. Also, if he took people out to sporting or other events, he would shoot two birds with one stone because he would be networking and enjoying himself at the same time.

One problem still stood, which was when to communicate with the list of contacts. He decided to schedule his day to start 30 minutes earlier at the office for email correspondences, then schedule another 30 minutes before lunch to make calls daily. He monitored his progress weekly (Appendix 4.1) to make sure that he connected with everyone on his contact list at least every other month. Scheduling networking contacts only added another five hours, which left him still with 26 hours a week of unadulterated freedom. Before itemizing his schedule, this time seemed unavailable. After Robert realized that it wouldn't take much more time to fit networking into the week, he was able to schedule this task like all the others and be on his way to building his client base.

Ted — 20yo, Perplexed Student

Once Ted was clear about breaking his mountainous tasks down to measurable molehills, scheduling them was a less daunting mission. Just as how he had to learn to plan tasks backward, he also had to schedule them backward from due date to the current date. This was the first priority any time he was given a new assignment or syllabus. However, whenever he put off scheduling, the amount of time he had for completing the task shortened. This was exactly what happened initially. Because this approach was unfamiliar, which meant it took some effort to formulate, Ted would procrastinate on breaking tasks down and scheduling them. Unfortunately, this resulted in a very familiar predicament: cramming at the last minute and producing subpar work quality.

To help Ted overcome this hump, we had to start by actually scheduling time for "breaking mountains into molehills" and scheduling. Ted spent an hour each morning for precisely this task. I educated him that this was essentially exercise for his brain. In order to develop new neuro-pathways for any foreign skill, he had to practice it repeatedly. The more he flexed those brain muscles, the stronger he would become. The more adept he became at applying the new skill, the less anxious he would be. Of course, this ultimately led to less procrastination, which was the main goal. After many weeks of practicing these scheduled skills, Ted became more efficient at scheduling. Furthermore, he realized that he actually had more free time to do as he pleased than before.

Ted used his phone and tablet for all of his scheduling, and made sure to sync up all devices at the end of each day. His digital planner gave him a visual representation of his day wherever he went and was easily updated on the go. Scheduling gave him a timeline of when an assignment or parts of it had to be done, so he could meet deadlines without pulling all-nighters. This flexibility reduced Ted's perfectionistic urge to have projects completed in one sitting devoid of breaks. It pushed him to be more proactive about his responsibilities without feeling overly anxious about them. He was still able to enjoy social activities with his peers while also accomplishing his academic workload. Plus, his free time became more enjoyable since he was productively getting the important things done too.

Julie – 45yo, Depleted Mom

One of the most important skills for Julie was retraining herself to abandon to-do lists in favor of scheduling. Prior to this, she made so many lists of chores and errands that she was actually spending more time making lists than doing what was listed. In fact, because there were so many lists, of which many were duplicates, seeing the pile of lists itself raised her anxiety level. We took items from every list, prioritized the urgency of each task, determined the time frame they needed, and slowly plugged them into the limited free time available in her planner. We also made sure to prioritize and schedule time for her newly created exercise regimen. However, there was another hiccup: Julie was having difficulty keeping up with the many changes to her daily schedule.

Having three young children meant that Julie had to be flexible and prepared for any curveball to her daily plans. In any given moment, she had to accommodate a sick child at home, pick up a hurt child from school, or attend to any imaginable emergency. With every unexpected situation that occurred requiring her immediate attention, a planned chore or errand had to be neglected. Over time, tasks in Julie's planner slowly became unplanned. Although Julie was doing an excellent job with scheduling, she didn't have a system to keep herself accountable. This was basically what happened with her to-do lists, and eventually, things piled up.

I instructed Julie to check items off of her schedule when they were completed, literally adding a checkmark or typing the word "done" next to the task. When items weren't accomplished during their scheduled times, they had to be rescheduled as soon as possible to the next available time before unscheduled items got lost in the shuffle. Of course, this sometimes meant having to push many tasks back if the one in question was of priority. Some chores that occurred daily or weekly, such as laundry or dishes, could easily be scheduled digitally on repeat mode and quickly be updated as needed. As Julie became more accustomed to this strategy, she began to feel less flustered and was less anxious overall. She felt more positive about herself and criticized herself less, as she began to see things getting done rather than merely listed. Not only had her productivity increased, she also made time for exercise and did it more days than not. The once-incomplete chores and errands became more manageable because she now had a scheduling system for her previously unproductive to-do lists.

As illustrated in these personal accounts, a detailed schedule will keep you on track to checking off completed tasks, while a vague schedule or no schedule will underrate your productive efforts. Each of these individuals has learned that only daily planners with specific time slots broken into 15-minute increments will suffice the objective of scheduling. Planners with monthly or weekly views are no different than to-do lists, and won't really hold you accountable to getting the job done if you are a serious procrastinator. Just as there are 168 hours in a week, there are 1,440 minutes in a day. Unless each of these valuable minutes is taken into account in your schedule, you will likely find time to procrastinate. It is much easier to let the minutes slip by while you aimlessly drag your feet than to put in the time and effort to achieve success.

Just as these individuals have learned, making a habit of breaking tasks down and scheduling them will initially take time. The more you flex those brain muscles and repeat the skill, the easier and more natural it becomes. As with any skill worth having, it will require effort. In addition, because today's smartphones allow you to have the ease of a calendar right at your fingertips, there really isn't a reason to not have a detailed schedule. And if you lose your phone, with modern syncing technology, you can still retrieve your schedule from any computer. So, you really have no excuse to not schedule your tasks immediately and be on your way to improved productivity ... unless you plan on failing.

CHAPTER FIVE

"When you rehearse success in your mind,
you experience it in your life."
—Remez Sasson

Jenny C. Yip, Psy.D., ABPP

From Visualization to Reality: The Five Senses

The final step in overcoming procrastination is to visualize yourself working through and completing your tasks every day. Think of it as muscle memory to achieve your goals. Your body and mind do not know the difference between an imagined experience and a real one. Remember the last time you had a nightmare? You probably woke up feeling terrified or possibly even screaming. Even though your dream is only imagined, your body and mind believe it to be reality. Visualizing your goals will supply you with the confidence that you *can* accomplish them, and encourage you to follow through on your plans. There are a number of key points to follow in order to make visualizations successful.

First, when you wake up in the morning, set aside 10 or 15 minutes to visualize all of your goals for that day. Visualize each precise task that you need to complete, using your scheduler as your guide. Don't simply recite to yourself that you need to clean your home. Instead, envision completing each of the tasks that you have scheduled in your planner for the day. Think through cleaning your kitchen, your bedroom, and your living room all separately. Doing this will make it clear to you how easily accomplishable your ultimate task of cleaning your home really is, and give you the belief that it can be done.

As you visualize each task, think about the details of accomplishing that particular goal. If you are visualizing cleaning your kitchen, imagine yourself scrubbing your sink and feeling the warm water and bubbly soapsuds run over your hands. Now you are wiping down the counter and scraping off all of the debris until the surface feels smooth to your touch. While mopping the floors, smell the pine freshness of the cleaning agent, and see the glistening shine as you feel the back-and-forth motion of the mop. Give yourself as many details as possible, and use all five of your senses to assist this process.

Providing details for completing your goals is like having road markers on a long journey. Without signs telling you how far you have come or what distance remains, you will easily become overwhelmed and worry that you may never reach the end. Having these "landmarks" allows you to pave the path you need to travel in order to reach your destination. Without this clear path, you will be lost without any direction to achieve your goal.

Again, make the visualization as realistic as possible, so that your mind and body cannot tell the difference from the real task. In every visualization, from the smallest tasks to the largest ones, imagine as many details of your environment and personal state as possible. Where are you? What colors are you wearing? Is it cold, hot, humid, dry? What sounds surround you? How does your dinner smell and taste? At the end, do you feel tired from a long day's work or rejuvenated by the particular task you've accomplished?

Most importantly, spend time envisioning and experiencing the completion of each molehill as well as the whole mountain. Even if you are working on a project that takes months – perhaps organizing a major account or losing a few pounds – include a visualization of yourself completing your long-term goals every single day. Imagine what it will be like putting that final touch on your project and the fulfilling, satisfying sensation of a job well done. I cannot emphasize how important it is to really *feel* the completion of your task. Act exactly as you would during the real situation.

If you envision scoring the game-winning shot, then feel the motion of your body as the ball travels from your hands through the air and toward the goal. Jump up and down with joy, and do a victory dance. Imagine your teammates surrounding you, patting you on the back and embracing you. What will the wind feel like as they carry you on their shoulders? If you are receiving a trophy, how will it feel in your hands, the cold metal pressed against your skin? When you really see and experience yourself completing a task, it makes your mind and body feel as if you have already accomplished it. The excitement from your achievement feels 100 percent real. This lets you believe that the work *is* achievable, and supplies you the confidence, motivation, and energy you need to push forward and succeed.

VISUALIZATIONS
5 Senses

THOUGHTS
"This is possible."

BEHAVIORS
Productivity

EMOTIONS
Excitement, Motivation

As you've already learned, a major contributor to procrastination is the inability to see the top of the mountain you are climbing. Visualizations overcome this by allowing you to mentally and emotionally experience the success that awaits you at the top of that mountain. Even more than this, they can provide you with the very experience of success. When you feel success is possible and can see success ahead, you will be more motivated toward actually putting in the effort to achieve it. Finishing any task is easier the second time around, whether it be simply cleaning your kitchen or putting the last touches on your novel. Visualizations give you the confidence of having already completed a task one or multiple times, even though it may actually be your very first time.

PERSONAL ANECDOTES

Raquel – 12yo, Piano Prodigy

To convert her negative fight-or-flight fear of playing poorly into positive excitement that energized her performance, Raquel utilized the visualization strategy for upcoming piano recitals. I instructed her to visualize each aspect of the performance: Waiting her turn behind the curtains and feeling her heart beat faster as the audience claps -- signaling the finale of the previous performer. Hearing the audience quiet down as she steps up on the vast stage to take her bow. Feeling the chill in the auditorium as she sits in front of the shiny, black grand piano to set up her music sheets. Taking a deep breath as she places her slightly trembling fingertips on the starting keys. Feeling her fingers lift and flow in feathery motion from key to key. Seeing and hearing the notes on the music sheet as she plays the associating keys effortlessly. Noticing the audience's captive focus as she presses the final keys to her performance. Feeling the heat within her hands and body that generated as she stands up to smile and bow again. Seeing the audience cheering and clapping with astonished faces, as she turns and disappears back behind the curtains.

Raquel visualized this sequence right before and after each piano rehearsal daily. Because of this, as the recital loomed closer, she felt more energized and excited to give the performance of her life. Although she still felt anxious, she understood that this was her body's fight-or-flight energy at work, and it was necessary to keep her motivated to practice and liven up the actual recital. Raquel also had to learn to visualize in the here and now, as if the recital was actually occurring in the present moment. This made the visualizations tangible and authentic. Each time she visualized the scene, new elements that weren't previously in her awareness was added. The more her visualizations became clearer and real, the more she believed that the goal was reachable. Over time, Raquel didn't only believe in the power of visualizations, she believed in her own skills because she mentally saw herself repeatedly deliver the performance without falter.

Robert – 30s, Ambitious Workaholic

Productivity wasn't Robert's main problem. Rather, the challenge was motivating him to focus his energy where needed to reach his goal of making partner at the firm. Other than presenting monthly financial reports and analyzing contracts, he now knew that he had to put time into building his client base to meet a specific quota. Since time spent networking was established as a necessity to bring more clients to the firm, this aspect of his job had to be prioritized. Yet Robert found every excuse in the book, though many were reasonable. It wasn't until his schedule was itemized that he began to consider the feasibility of time afforded to networking. To reinforce the importance of this agenda, we examined the short- and long-term costs and benefits (Appendix 5.2) of time spent networking. Through this process, it was determined that visualization was one of the key strategies that facilitated his goal, and the long-term benefits far outweighed the costs.

Accordingly, I had him spend 10 minutes every morning visualizing what it would be like to make partner at the firm. He had to imagine every detail: his importance and prestige; how highly he would be regarded by his peers; how his opinions would be valued. I asked him to imagine his appearance: the power suit and tie; the polished dress shoe; his slicked-back hair; the new leather briefcase. He was also to imagine other areas of his life affected by this promotion. He could spend more time on important tasks and delegate the menial duties to other associates. This would give him even more time to network to bring in additional clients. As his status increased, he would also have more free time whenever he wanted it, rather than when it was granted by his work obligations.

Through these daily visualizations, Robert felt excited about the success of becoming partner. Imagining it happening triggered the sense that it was possible and within reach. This, in turn, energized him to strive to overcome the obstacle that stood in the way: lack of time spent on networking to build his client base. And so, whenever it came time to email correspondences or make calls to touch base with colleagues and clients, he carried the tasks out with enthusiasm rather than annoyance. In his mind, he was on his way to making partner at the firm.

Ted – 20yo, Perplexed Student

To hold Ted accountable to his daily schedules, he had to apply visualizations to foster the "I can" attitude. Otherwise, Ted became anxious and overwhelmed whenever he glanced over his digital planner and realized the 101 tasks he, like most college students, was responsible for. For Ted, it was crucial to use the visualization strategy every morning just after waking up and every night before bedtime. This kept him on track with positive fight-or-flight energy versus dread, because visualizing the completion of each task on his daily planner made the task possible and doable. Since it was feasible in his mind, he realized it was also viable in real life. The important aspect was to use all five of his senses during the visualizations: to see, hear, feel, smell, and taste the success of completing each task in his schedule accordingly.

Ted used the Visualization Tracking Worksheet (Appendix 5.1) to monitor his thoughts, emotions, and resulting productivity level when visualizations were used to reach a goal. What he observed was a substantial increase in his academic productivity. The satisfaction Ted felt from actually accomplishing tasks without having to cram last minute was exactly the sensation he strived for during each visualization. He imagined executing the task from start to finish and every detail involved in the process. To lessen his usual perfectionistic tendency to complete long projects in one sitting, which led to anxiety and procrastination, he was instructed to visualize the final product in addition to the immediate task at hand. This part-to-whole visualization strategy helped him see each landmark along the path to project completion without absurdly believing that it all had to be finished in order to achieve perfect results.

To practice tolerating imperfection, I also had Ted imagine making errors along the way, and problem-solving for the flaws if it was possible. I reminded him that such mistakes were opportunities to learn and progress. Otherwise, there wouldn't be room for improvement if things were already perfect. As such, he wouldn't grow and evolve. Visualizing daily responsibilities from his planner helped to decrease Ted's anxiety about getting them done. Seeing the outcome showed him that he *can* do it. He was no longer feeling overwhelmed by the mountainous tasks. Rather, he felt satisfied from the success of tackling each scheduled molehill one by one.

Julie – 45yo, Depleted Mom

Doing visualizations each morning helped Julie organize her daily chores and errands mentally. As she saw the sequence of each task completion, she paved the roadmap of her responsibilities each day from start to finish. She knew exactly what to look for, where to stop, which corner to turn, and so on and so forth. This increased her efficiency during the limited free time she had when her three kids didn't need her immediate attention. Rather than wasting time searching and debating which task from her to-do list was priority, she knew from her visualizations exactly what had to be done and in what order. When she forgot the next task, all she had to do was look at the map on her planner.

Most chores and errands were fairly familiar to Julie, since she had previously completed them many times. However, she had to expend more energy focusing her five senses on scheduled exercises. In her visualizations, Julie would feel her heart rate increase, hear her heavy breathing, smell odors of sweat, see her muscles flexing, and taste liquids that quenched her thirst. She had to feel the soreness and tightness of the next day, which indicated that the hard labor was worth her body's time. More importantly, her daily visualizations concluded with images of her transformed body, improved endurance, and overall expanded energy, which was her main goal.

Experiencing the transformation mentally truly motivated Julie to go after the change in real life, because it became tangible. Instead of feeling distressed by the seemingly never-ending to-do lists, there was a definite end to each task as she imagined its completion. Each exercise regimen completed advanced her to the next benchmark in her workout endeavor. Focusing her five senses on the outcomes increased her energy to work toward them. In turn, seeing actual results propelled her to continue on the path to success. Chores, errands, and exercise became targets to achieve in order to feel rewarded, rather than appearing like laborious tasks that she was once forced to complete. This shift in perspective gave her a more positive outlook to each day, where she no longer woke up dreading the day ahead. By visualizing with her five senses, she was checking tasks off mentally, which enabled her to actually check them off literally.

Visualizations can transform discouraging situations into attainable successes. As experienced by each of these individuals, before utilizing visualizations, their days seem like a towering mountain that must be slowly pushed up, inch-by-inch, without ever reaching the top. After learning to use visualizations, they feel more positive about accomplishing their goals because they have already mentally experienced the triumph of completing them. In turn, the feeling of achievement further enhances an "I can" attitude to continue striving for productive success. Once a pile of burdens has now become a path of reachable possibilities.

The ingredients to any effective visualization include: integrating specific details, combining all five senses, and envisioning the completion of the goal. Whether you are looking to accomplish mundane daily tasks or long-term aspirations, visualizations will allow you to feel the success of your efforts, and thus, motivate you to actually achieve them. Just as many athletes train through visualizations to improve their performances, so can you to improve your productivity. Like these individuals, you too can start each day with excitement toward achieving your goals and dreams, rather than kicking and screaming over the mountainous tasks in your way. When you visualize success, it becomes more attainable, simply because your mind believes it. This is your mental rehearsal at work. Use it regularly, because being productive is certainly a more rewarding experience.

CHAPTER SIX

"Nothing great was ever achieved
without enthusiasm."
–Ralph Waldo Emerson

Congratulations to The Productive, Successful YOU!

In the first section of this book, you have learned how the fight-or-flight response impacts your motivation: You can become overwhelmed and anxious or underwhelmed and unmotivated. You have learned how distorted thoughts contribute to your interpretation of what the fight-or-flight alarm means. To become productive, you must use the fight-or-flight energy to your advantage. You can identify your thinking errors and correct them so that your thoughts represent reality more accurately, minimizing your tendency to procrastinate.

In the second section of this book, you have learned specific tools and strategies that, when adapted to and practiced, will stop procrastination. You have learned how to break vague mountains into distinct objective molehills that are easily achievable. Thus, you can now create a path of clear landmarks that pave the direction to your destination – the completion of a task. You have learned the importance of scheduling each of these molehills in order to establish realistic deadlines for their completion. So, you can set a pace that will commit you to achieve each objective and reach your ultimate goal. Finally, you have learned how visualizations help you to travel the path that leads to your goal in order to feel the task is accomplishable. As a result, you understand how important it is to actually see, hear, touch, smell, and taste the success so you believe it's possible.

The tools you have begun to acquire will help you achieve and become the successful person you have always desired to be. As you practice and master these tools, you will wake up each day with the confidence and motivation to work toward your dreams ... if you can call it "work" anymore. You will have direction and a sense of purpose as you move toward your goals, while taking pleasure in your efforts each step along the way. As you reach your destination, you'll look back and be amazed at your efficiency in tackling the mountainous mission you set forth to accomplish, while thinking, "Whew … what a ride!"

Many people know me to be an ambitious thinker. When I imagine my future, it's limitless. My dreams and aspirations are only limited by what I think I *can* accomplish. Since there is no limit to what I can achieve once I set my mind to it, the possibilities are also endless. I start and end every day visualizing the path to my goal, whether immediate or long-term, seeing each landmark along the way. This imbues me with excitement about my future, and gives me the drive to be productive. In fact, I love what I do so much that most of the time it doesn't even feel like "work." Certainly, for those tasks that are more arduous and less enjoyable, I am even more diligent about implementing these tools.

The methods I have shared are strategies that I've developed over many years to reach my successes. Because perseverance and achievement were highly valued traits in my upbringing, I had to find ways to be as productive as humanly possible. As with any curious child, I tested this and tried that to determine what worked best. With each new task or assignment, I quickly adapted to the strategies that were effective and abandoned the ones that weren't. Over time, this set of skills accumulated and became innate and automatic.

Many of my patients have also used these same strategies to overcome procrastination and improve their productivity. Now you can do the same. Since the possibilities are limitless, my mission remains open-ended and nowhere near complete. I have many more aspirations to fulfill in the years to come, and will continue applying these tools to reach each and every one of them. If I can do it, so can you. Congratulations!

PERSONAL ANECDOTES

Raquel – 12yo, Piano Prodigy

Although Raquel had spent most of her childhood playing the piano, recitals became nerve-racking as her worries about performing poorly increased. Her hands would shake and sweat whenever she thought about having to play piano in front of an audience. Consequently, she began to procrastinate to avoid feeling the intense anxiety upon each imminent threat of a recital performance. She was no longer having fun because she felt piano practice became more work than play. Her irrational drive to give a perfect performance at each recital also didn't help to lessen this burden. She was consumed with such negative thoughts like "I won't be able to play perfectly," and "People will laugh at me," that her anxiety was often heightened during the week of recitals.

Rather than falsely attributing the value of dangerous sabertooth tiger to piano recitals, Raquel learned to interpret her body's natural fight-or-flight alarm as positive excitement necessary for a lively performance. As uncomfortable as it may be, she had to accept that her body needed some sense of urgency to motivate her to practice to perform well. Raquel also spent a great deal of time understanding how perception was shaped by personal biases rather than factual reality. As such, she had the ability to perceive the fight-or-flight response as useful energy, if that was what she chose.

In order to eliminate her unproductive, perfectionistic thinking pattern, Raquel learned to tackle cognitive distortions that trapped her in procrastination mode. This taught her to rely on evidence based on her skills and past performances, as opposed to her biased beliefs. We also lightened the "work" of recital practice by breaking down mountainous rehearsals and adding molehills of free-play for fun. These smaller molehills were scheduled in a detailed planner to keep Raquel on track for accomplishing the established goals efficiently within the set timeframes.

Finally, to add the cherry to the topping and foster genuine confidence in her own abilities, Raquel learned to visualize the details of her recital as if it was happening in the moment. Mentally experiencing a successful performance transformed her fight-or-flight anxiety into productive energy to practice rather than procrastinate. Because of her efforts, she gave one successful recital after another, all the while interpreting her body's natural fight-or-flight trigger beneficially.

Robert – 30s, Ambitious Workaholic

Robert was a young, hard-working attorney with one main goal: to make partner at the law firm, and one main problem: monthly presentations that gave him anxiety attacks.

Yet, rather than considering the overall criteria for making partner, he placed too much emphasis on possible negative evaluations from his superiors. Thus, he spent excessively more time perfecting these monthly financial reports at the expense of lowered productivity in other areas of his job. Part of this was due to the fact that it would take him a whole week to recover from energy wasted after giving each report. In addition, despite his conviction that he was immune to thinking fallacies, Robert was like all of us – preys of thought traps that flew under the radar. Specifically, he had many thoughts related to perceived incompetency that triggered his anxiety attacks.

Robert had to learn to balance his fight-or-flight energy to stabilize his overall productive momentum and avoid eventual burnout. Only when he was able to accept that he, too, committed cognitive distortions was he able to examine his thought sequence rationally. He constantly had to choose efficiency versus accuracy in his thinking pattern, and challenged negative thoughts that kept him from optimal productivity by questioning their accuracy. Through this process, Robert realized that the most logical path to reach his goal was to spread his energy evenly across his workload.

In addition, rather than wandering aimlessly to reach the vague, mountainous goal of becoming partner, Robert learned that he needed to spend time building his client base. He established several measurable sub-goals and scheduled each strategy into his planner. By breaking down and itemizing his weekly commitments, he also realized he could afford the time for networking obligations in order to bring more clients to the firm. Finally, in order to redirect his energy and help him realize his main goal, Robert spent valuable time daily visualizing himself as a partner at the firm. Once he saw a path to his ultimate destination, he was able to productively direct his efforts according to the roadmap.

Ted – 20yo, Perplexed Student

Since starting college, Ted was dumbfounded about his once-4.0 GPA from high school. He wasn't used to the lack of strict structure and direction that was inherent to college academics. Because of his lack of clarity and planning skills, he was constantly in procrastination mode from feeling intensely anxious about big projects and final exams. One of his main obstacles was to overcome his perfectionistic tendency to have each assignment completed in one sitting, which was what he was accustomed to in high school. However, with college assignments that tended to take a substantial amount of time to complete, he often felt paralyzed by the mountainous tasks, without having the skills necessary to break them down. As his frustration level increased, so did his negative self-talk. Yet, rather than problem-solving for his sliding grades, he resorted to further procrastination, which felt safer in the moment.

Ted trained his mind to take control of the vicious procrastination – cramming cycle by confronting the problem rather than avoiding it. He learned to tackle self-defeating thoughts that inhibited his confidence to challenge the sabertooth. He accomplished this by using his fight-or-flight discomfort to signal the possibility of cognitive distortions that flew by. As his awareness of these thought traps improved, so did his ability to decipher false alarms from actual threats.

Ted also acquired the necessary skill of breaking mountainous tasks down to measurable steps by learning to plan backward. Once he was able to see each sequential step from task completion to task initiation, he no longer felt the need to have everything completed singlehandedly. Scheduling these molehills allowed him to see a definite end to each particular phase, while moving in a specified direction. Rather than feeling exhausted by the perceived never-ending tasks, the roadmaps gave him reachable landmarks and guidance to accomplish each assignment. In addition, daily visualizations fostered the "I can" attitude, since he mentally saw himself completing each task, big and small, from his planner. After spending many weeks training his mind to flex the newly developed brain muscles, the whole approach became less intimidating. As Ted's anxiety about vague, unstructured assignments decreased, so did his procrastination.

Julie – 45yo, Depleted Mom

Being a sleep-deprived, stay-at-home mom with three young children, Julie had a difficult time completing the numerous household chores, tasks, and errands from her many to-do lists. During her limited free time, she was usually too exhausted or unmotivated to check items off of these lists. This was no different than her many attempted exercise plans. However, each time she felt unproductive, she wasted mental energy punishing herself with self-blame that upset her even further. Not only did this decrease her motivation to exercise and tackle her to-do lists, she felt burdened by the seemingly unfulfilling obligations.

Julie had to understand that much of her fight-or-flight energy was spent on her children's care, where it was needed. Thus, when it came to her to-do lists, they took the backseat of importance. By breaking down each task from her lists and assigning practical timeframes every task needed, she realized that she wasn't as unproductive as she had imagined. In fact, she learned to break free from these irrational thought traps by giving herself justified credit for accomplishing as much as she did in a day's time. She also found exercises that were enjoyable and that could be slowly integrated into her schedule.

In addition, Julie abandoned the ineffective to-do list in favor of a detailed planner that was flexible enough to accommodate her constantly changing schedule. She prioritized tasks and exercises, and assigned them to specific timeframes in her planner. Every morning, she visualized the sequence of each chore and errand to pave the roadmap for the day ahead. As Julie's expectations became more realistic, so were her thoughts about her capacity. In turn, she felt more positive about herself and became increasingly energized to complete her scheduled tasks. As a result, feeling rewarded from checking items off of her daily schedule motivated her to stay on this formulated path to continued productivity. What once triggered anxiety now provided her with the sense of success.

For Raquel, Robert, Ted, and Julie, what previously seemed a mere possibility had transformed into an inevitable reality. Before learning to use these tools, they were overwhelmed, overworked, and overstressed and found themselves procrastinating or lacking productivity. Self-imposed goals that weren't reached only contributed to negative self-talk, more anxiety, and further procrastination. By making use of their natural fight-or-flight trigger for energy and motivation, challenging cognitive distortions, breaking mountains into molehills, scheduling, and visualizing, each person has accomplished more than what they normally would have for the same amount of time and dedication.

Nevertheless, even with all of these tools at their fingertips, being productive is not just a walk in the park. It takes hard work and dedication to achieve any goal. As you have read, it may seem easier to not put in the effort to become productive in the short-term. However, in the long run, you're wreaking havoc on your body -- mentally, emotionally, and physically -- with unnecessary anxiety if you would rather procrastinate than get things done.

The tools that are now within your reach will reduce this anxiety, and motivate you to achieve the goals that you truly *want* to accomplish. Whether for immediate mundane tasks or long-term ambitions, these strategies will get you there if you put them to use in your daily life. As you notice changes to your productivity, give yourself a pat on your shoulder and congratulate yourself for taking the exciting path to success as these individuals have.

EPILOGUE

"The question isn't who is going to let me;
it's who is going to stop me."
—Ayn Rand

A Final Word of Encouragement ...

At the end of the day, you are what you make of yourself. You can choose to discount everything you've read. You can keep making excuses for why these tools will not work. You can continue procrastinating your life away. Or here is another option: Experiment with what you've learned in this book. Test out your experience of the fight-or-flight response, and see if you can make the adrenaline rush work effectively for you. Take time to identify those cognitive distortions and correct them, so they can't hold you prisoner to procrastination. Break those ginormous, vague tasks into smaller, well-defined goals that you can easily reach. Make the effort to schedule each individual goal into a working planner so you have landmarks and deadlines for completing your tasks. Lastly, feel the success by actually visualizing every detail and step to your final accomplishment.

If you take the time to practice each of these tools, then you too can overcome procrastination. There is no magic solution. There is no quick fix. Disciplining yourself to be productive takes time and training. This, like most journeys in life, is a process. With the right attitude and dedication, you can reach your goals and become the productive, successful "YOU." Put these tools to action and make your anxiety work *for* you rather than against you! What else have you got to lose, except time?

I don't know about you, however, I certainly don't want to be lying in my deathbed one day regretting all the opportunities I've missed because I procrastinated!

As you adapt to these tools ... or not, perhaps you will take a moment and send me a quick note about your progress. I would love to read your thoughts, suggestions, what worked for you or didn't. All your feedback will help to improve the next edition. As I've once said, it takes a great student to make a teacher great! Without your insights, I would not have much to teach.

Now, this is your journey … Make it one you will not regret!

Welcome to the productive, successful you!

APPENDIX

Your Next-Action Checklist

___ **Appendix 1.1 & 1.2**

Notice your experience of the fight-or-flight response. Identify your emotional reaction to the adrenaline rush. What is the result when you interpret it as excitement versus anxiety? Are you able to distinguish the difference between the objective sensations and the subjective emotional experience? Make the adrenaline rush work effectively for you by utilizing this energy toward productive goals.

___ **Appendix 2.1 & 2.2**

Take the time to identify your cognitive distortions and correct them, so they can't hold you prisoner to procrastination. Use your procrastination habits or feelings of anxiety as red flags to check for distortions in your thought patterns. Does evidence exist that supports your thoughts? If not, determine alternative interpretations that reflect reality more accurately to eliminate unproductive thoughts and actions.

___ **Appendix 3.1 & 3.2**

Break your ginormous, vague tasks into smaller, well-defined goals that you can easily reach. Clarify your roadmap by planning backward from the end goal. Determine each sequential step and the timeframes needed for each step. What are the strategies required to reach each step and potential obstacles along the way? Anticipate alternative pathways as possible resolutions to maintain your route toward the ultimate goal.

Appendix 4.1 & 4.2

Schedule each individual goal into a working planner so you have landmarks and deadlines for completing your tasks. Do you have a planner that you can easily use and have with you at all times? Are you able to schedule small enough increments (15 minutes)? Make sure to update your schedule regularly, and immediately reschedule incomplete tasks to ensure they're accounted for so you can focus on being productive.

Appendix 5.1 & 5.2

Feel your success by visualizing every detail and step to your final accomplishment. Do your visualizations include all five of your senses so you can experience the path to your destination as realistic as possible? Are you using your schedule every morning to guide you in visualizing completing each precise task for the day and the ultimate goal? Experience the confidence, motivation, and energy as you see yourself reaching your goal and feeling the satisfaction of success.

APPENDIX 1.1

Fight-or-Flight Awareness Checklist

OBJECTIVE PHYSIOLOGICAL SENSATIONS	SUBJECTIVE EMOTIONAL EXPERIENCES *(Unproductive) (Productive)*	
Increased heart rate	*Alarm*	*Alertness*
Headaches, muscle tension	*Unfocused*	*Concentrated*
Lightheadedness, nausea	*Disoriented*	*Sharpness*
Shaking or restlessness	*Helplessness*	*Activated*
Tightness in the chest	*Worry*	*Drive*
Shortness of breath	*Discouraged*	*Inspired*
Dry mouth or lump in the throat	*Dread*	*Motivated*
Tingling or numbness in parts of the body	*Vulnerable*	*Vigor*
Sweaty or clammy skin	*Being on edge*	*Endurance*
Stomach problems or sudden diarrhea	*Anxiety*	*Excitement*
Flushes or chills	*Fatigue*	*Energized*

Fight-or-Flight Thermometer

10	Overextension, straining energy, breaking point, procrastination
9	Distraught, distressing energy, overwhelmed, procrastination
8	Threatening, excessive energy, maximum productivity, cramming
7	Alarm, superior energy, high productivity
6	Warning, intense energy, enhanced productivity
5	Alert, moderate energy, modest productivity
4	Caution, mild energy, minimal productivity
3	Aware, diminutive energy, negligible productivity
2	Relaxed, complacent, no productivity
1	Bored, underwhelmed, no productivity, procrastination
0	Dead, no reflex

APPENDIX 1.2

Objective Sensation vs. Subjective Experience Log

OBJECTIVE PHYSIOLOGICAL SENSATION	THERMOMETER LEVEL	SUBJECTIVE EMOTIONAL EXPERIENCE	RESULTING ACTION

APPENDIX 2.1

Cognitive Distortion Thought Record (Sample)

DISTORTED THOUGHT	COGNITIVE ERRORS	CONTRADICTING EVIDENCE	ALTERNATIVE THOUGHT
"I always procrastinate, so there's no point in getting started."	All or Nothing Irrelevant Connection	Just because I have a history of procrastinating doesn't mean I have to keep letting it happen.	"Habits can be changed. Even if I do just a little bit of work, I would still be getting something done to reach my goal."
"Many people procrastinate and still do well, so it doesn't really matter that I do it."	Overgeneralization Irrelevant Connection	I am my own person, accountable for my own actions, and am not defined by other people. What other people do doesn't determine what I do.	"I don't have to procrastinate like everyone else. I may even do better than everyone else if I plan and complete my work before last minute deadline."
"My boss thinks I'm a slacker. Even if I put in the time, I'll still fail."	Jumping to Conclusions Labeling	I can't read anyone's mind, and I don't have a crystal ball to see into the future.	"I can put in the needed time to complete the task, so I won't give my boss reason to believe I'm a slacker."
"I don't know why my parents make me play the violin. They should know how much I really hate practicing when I already have so much to do."	Reverse Mind Reading Should Statement	No one can read my mind. I can't expect other people to know what I'm thinking if I don't tell them.	"I'll tell my parents that I don't enjoy the violin, because I don't have time to practice with all of my other academic responsibilities."

"I'll be fired unless I give this presentation perfectly."	Catastrophizing Jumping to Conclusions All or Nothing	What's perfect to me may not be perfect to others, and I don't have a crystal ball to see into the future.	"I need to schedule time to rehearse this presentation, so I can minimize awkwardness during the real thing."
"If I don't get this presentation just perfect, I'll be the laughing stock of my group,"	Magnification All or Nothing Jumping to Conclusions	Nothing is perfect, and I don't know how other people will respond.	"Giving an imperfect presentation doesn't mean my group will laugh at me. They might not even notice my minor imperfections."
"It really won't make a difference in my marathon training if I miss just this one day of practice."	Minimization Exceptional Rule Justification	Every little bit of training has an effect on the overall result.	"If I miss this day of practice, then I have to accept that my marathon training may be negatively impacted."
"I've only finished one assignment; I'll never get through the other five."	Mental Filter Jumping to Conclusions	Finishing one is better than none. I don't know that I won't finish the other five assignments.	"I am one step closer to completing all of my assignments."
"I'm no genius... I just got lucky."	Discounting the Positives Minimization	Luck still requires reaching opportunities to be at the right place at the right time.	"Even minor efforts accumulate to achieve results."
"If I watch a little TV now and pull an all-nighter to finish this paper, I would still meet the morning deadline and wouldn't really be procrastinating."	Exceptional Rule Justification Minimization Irrelevant Connection	Procrastination is procrastination no matter what the results are.	"If I work on this paper now, then I won't have to pull an all-nighter to meet the morning deadline. I may even have a little time for TV afterwards."

"It's okay to procrastinate a little on this proposal for now, because I am too distracted with emails at the moment."	Irrelevant Connection Minimization	Procrastination is procrastination no matter what the reasons are.	"Being distracted with other tasks doesn't permit me to procrastinate. If I put aside my distractions, then I can concentrate on this proposal."
"I'm feeling too tired to work on this project, so it's best that I put it off until I feel more energetic to produce amazing results."	Emotional Reasoning Irrelevant Connection	What I feel doesn't have to determine what I do. Tiredness can be remedied with a power nap, short break, or caffeine.	"If I take a quick 20min nap, then I'll be more refreshed to power through this project."
"I still haven't started my project; I'm a failure."	Labeling Personalization and Blame All or Nothing	Labeling flaws with negative names doesn't reflect the situation accurately or help to improve it.	"If I break this project down into molehills and schedule it now, then I can visualize the completion and achieve my goal."
"Because Sheila distracted me, I haven't finished any of my work!"	Personalization and Blame Magnification	I can't hold anyone accountable for my actions except myself.	"I need to move away from Sheila's distraction so I can stay focused on my work."
"I should have finished this earlier."	Should Statements Personalization and Blame	Blame is negative, unnecessary, and doesn't help any situation.	"I'll put this in my planner now, so I'll get to it and finish it as scheduled."

APPENDIX 2.2

Cognitive Distortion Thought Record

DISTORTED THOUGHT	COGNITIVE ERRORS	CONTRADICTING EVIDENCE	ALTERNATIVE THOUGHT

APPENDIX 3.1

Breaking Mountains into Molehills Clarification Map

Identify a project that feels insurmountable or overwhelming whenever you think about it.

GOAL: _____

_____

Determine how you can break this project down into smaller, tangible steps until each step feels reachable when you think about it.

STEP #1: _____

_____

Develop **specific** and **detailed** strategies to reach each step, so the steps *feel* easy to you when you think about them.

STRATEGY #1: _____

_____

STRATEGY #2: _____

_____

STEP #2: _____

_____

STRATEGY #1: _____

_____

STRATEGY #2: _____

_____

STEP #3: _____

_____

STRATEGY #1: _____

_____

STRATEGY #2: _____

_____

APPENDIX 3.2

Stepwise Goal Planner

		STRATEGIES	TIME FRAME	POTENTIAL OBSTACLES	POSSIBLE RESOLUTIONS
GOAL #1	Healthcare Reform Paper	Brainstorm 4 possible topics	30mins		
		Outline thesis statement and 3 supporting arguments	30mins	No research data supporting arguments	Do literature review to determine validity of thesis or establish new thesis
		Write sections for intro, supporting arguments, conclusion	1hr / section		
GOAL #2					
GOAL #3					
GOAL #4					

APPENDIX 4.1

Task Monitoring Checklist

GOAL/TASK	SCHEDULE DATE/TIME	ACHIEVED RESCHEDULED	OUTCOME
Brainstorm 4 possible topics	Yes	Achieved	Completed
Outline thesis statement and 3 supporting arguments	Yes	No research data Rescheduled	Completed after literature review
Write sections for intro, supporting arguments, conclusion	Yes	Achieved	Completed after spending another 30mins for final edits.

APPENDIX 4.2

Daily Task Planner

TIME	MONDAY	TUESDAY	WEDNESDAY
6 am			
:15			
:30			
:45			
7 am			
:15			
:30			
:45			
8 am			
:15			
:30			
:45			
9 am			
:15			
:30			
:45			
10 am			
:15			
:30			
:45			
11 am			
:15			
:30			
:45			
12 pm			
:15			
:30			
:45			
1 pm			
:15			
:30			
:45			
2 pm			
:15			
:30			
:45			
3 pm			
:15			
:30			
:45			
4 pm			
:15			
:30			
:45			
5 pm			
:15			
:30			
:45			
6 pm			
:15			
:30			
:45			

Daily Task Planner

TIME	THURSDAY	FRIDAY	SATURDAY
6 am			
:15			
:30			
:45			
7 am			
:15			
:30			
:45			
8 am			
:15			
:30			
:45			
9 am			
:15			
:30			
:45			
10 am			
:15			
:30			
:45			
11 am			
:15			
:30			
:45			
12 pm			
:15			
:30			
:45			
1 pm			
:15			
:30			
:45			
2 pm			
:15			
:30			
:45			
3 pm			
:15			
:30			
:45			
4 pm			
:15			
:30			
:45			
5 pm			
:15			
:30			
:45			
6 pm			
:15			
:30			
:45			

APPENDIX 5.1

Visualization Tracking Worksheet

DATE TIME	5 SENSES VISUALIZATION	THOUGHT	EMOTION	PRODUCTIVITY RESULT
8/1/12 AM	Yes *(Research and brainstorm 4 possible topics. Outline thesis statement and 3 supporting arguments.)*	It's clear what I need to research, so the outline can be easily prepared.	Motivated. Achievable goal.	Completed brainstorm & outline in 75mins. Need to adjust schedule. Feeling satisfied & productive.
8/2/12 AM	Yes *(Opening box of CDs I self-produced. Appearance & feel of album. Smell of packaging. Feeling successful from recording 1st album.)*	I can't wait to finish the 1st step in my journey of being a musician. I can make this my reality.	Excitement. Energetic to get working.	Mixed first 2 songs and finished rehearsing track #3. Ready to schedule actual recording for tomorrow. Feeling successful & confident in reaching my dreams.

APPENDIX 5.2

The question is do you really want to change? By reading this book to the end, you've demonstrated a strong desire for change. People who say they *can't* change usually mean they don't want to put in the effort to change. Change is difficult because it involves time, energy, and commitment without a guarantee for positive results. At the end of the day, we are creatures of habit. And it may *feel* easier to continue the same old habit than to commit to change. Or is it? Is the long term benefit worth the short term sacrifice? Is the short-term gain actually costing more in the long run? To generate clarity into the reasons for change, it's necessary to determine the pros and cons for the consequences of our actions... or lack of.

Costs & Benefits Analysis

Goals	Productivity Strategy	Costs		Benefits	
		Short-Term	Long-Term	Short-Term	Long-Term
Preparing a 2-hr PowerPoint workshop	Breaking mountains into molehills	Tedious & time-consuming.	Takes time away from more enjoyable activities in life.	I'll be less anxious, because I'll have a plan of action. The end product will be of higher quality.	The skill will become 2nd nature the more it's practiced
Final research paper edits	Scheduling & visualizations	Takes even more effort.	Feels too rigid to have all of my tasks scheduled.	I'll feel confident about my ability to complete the edits, so I can get it done w/o procrastination.	Productivity will improve as I get use to the tools and turn them into habits.

ABOUT JENNY C. YIP, PSY.D., ABPP

Jenny C. Yip, Psy.D., ABPP, is a clinical psychologist, author, speaker, and a nationally recognized obsessive-compulsive disorder (OCD) and anxiety expert. She developed the Family Systems-Based Strategic CBT, and has successfully treated severe OCD and anxiety disorders for over a decade.

In 2008, Dr. Yip established the Renewed Freedom Center in Los Angeles to help those suffering from OCD and anxiety disorders by providing the most advanced treatment available. She is Board Certified in Cognitive & Behavioral Psychology by the American Board of Professional Psychology (ABPP), and is a Clinical Assistant Professor of Psychiatry at the USC Keck School of Medicine.

Inspired by her own struggles and triumph with OCD since childhood, Dr. Yip is tirelessly involved in a range of organizational, educational, and media projects to raise awareness and eliminate negative stigmas about mental health.